GAME CHANGERS

Going Local to Defeat
Violent Extremists

ABRIDGED CITIZEN'S EDITION

By:

Lieutenant Colonel (Retired)
D. Scott Mann (Special Forces)

D1508807

Craig,

Thanks for your
service & courage
Brother, DOL

Scott
Ma—

Game Changers:
Going Local to Defeat Violent Extremists
Abridged Citizen's Edition

Published by Tribal Analysis Center of Leesburg, Virginia.

ISBN-13:
978-1978442979

ISBN-10:
1978442971

Editor: Mark Tompkins
Layout: Andrea Reider
Cover: Arthur Angelo
Illustrations: R. Keene
Production and Publication Support: Ignite Press
www.ignitepress.co

Library of Congress Control Number: 2015941724

Visit our websites:
www.Rooftopleadership.com
www.tribalanalysiscenter.com
www.stabilityinstitute.com
www.thegamechangersbook.com

Tribal Analysis Publishing

The Department of Defense Office of Pre-Publication and
Security Review has cleared this book for publication.

To Monty and the "Mann cubs" — Cody, Cooper, and Brayden.

Your quiet sacrifice and enduring love during this long war
inspired me more than you'll ever know.

Contents

PART I: Defining the Game 1

    Chapter 1: Introduction 3

    Chapter 2: Why We Are Losing 7

    Chapter 3: Where the Pavement Ends 19

    Chapter 4: Square Tank in a Round Jirga 31

PART II: CHANGING THE GAME 41

    Chapter 5: Finding Lawrence 43

    Chapter 6: The Game Changer Framework 55

    Chapter 7: Getting Surrounded 73
    (Village Stability Operations)

    Chapter 8: Meet Them Where They Are — 85
    Embracing Local Realities

    Chapter 9: Extreme Collaboration: 97
    It Takes a Village and a Network

    Chapter 10: Lead with Story 115

PART III: Into Action 135

    Chapter 11: Bypassing the Graveyard 137

    Chapter 12: No Respite: Islamist Violent 153
    Extremists in the Homeland

    Chapter 13: Conclusion 163

NOTES 169

BIBLIOGRAPHY 181

ABOUT THE AUTHOR 191

MAPS AND CHARTS

Figure 2-1   Map of Islamic Caliphate Expansion 7

Figure 3-1   Afghan Relative Stability Diagram................................ 22

Figure 3-2   Afghan Community Institutions Degraded.................... 27

Figure 3-3   Violent Extremist Exploitation of Clan Society 29

Figure 6-1   Game Changer Spectrum of Conflict 66

Figure 6-2   Game Changer Framework... 69

Figure 9-1   Iceberg of Society 107

Figure 10-1   The Power of Story in Both Societies..........................119

PREFACE

"The success of democracy depends, in the end, on the reliability of the judgments we citizens make, and hence upon our capacity and determination to weigh arguments and evidence rationally."

— Irving M. Copi

When my dear friend, Greg Smith suggested over lunch that I write an abridged version of *Game Changers* just a few years after releasing the original, I am embarrassed to say I snickered in his face.

"Greg, it took me over three years to write a book on this war that politicians, warriors, and cops can use to learn from the past - it was the hardest project I've ever done in life - why on earth would I do this again?!"

"Because we'll lose if you don't." Greg didn't flinch as he leveled his gaze at me. "Our politicians are not going to win this thing until our people demand that they do. And right now, there isn't enough information out there to inform citizens and activate them. You need to explain it."

Damn.

I knew he was right. I'd seen three U.S. Presidents, countless politicians and waves of policy makers wring their hands and half-heartedly bumble through the longest war in our Nation's history.

My son Cody was three when the towers fell, and as I write this, he's 19 and only two years from being commissioned into the U.S. Army - to go fight the war that his Dad didn't finish. With your children at his side, he'll fight this long war with the same failed strategy I had.

Unless you - the Citizen - demand a change.

With that in mind, I humbly offer you, Game Changers, the Citizens Guide to going local and defeating violent extremists.

I pray it serves you - and our Nation.

De Oppresso Liber.

FOREWORD

On October 1, 2014, Admiral Mike Mullen appeared as a guest on *The Colbert Report* on the Comedy Central cable channel. At one point in the interview the host, Stephen Colbert, in a serious vein, asked Admiral Mullen, "Do you ever get tired of the Middle East ... of all the different fires we're having to put out?"

The former Chairman of the Joint Chiefs gave an answer that struck me as extremely significant and, in fact, disturbingly revelatory:

ADMIRAL MULLEN

What I would like to see is ... an overarching strategy and plan for the Middle East, country by country and then even in the regional sense ... and I think having that ... would then allow everybody to figure out how they could contribute, if it's another country, or how we could contribute even inside our own country.

A strategy and a plan.

In other words, a vision.

We, the United States, clearly do not have one, or Admiral Mullen would not have phrased his answer the way that he did.

The 21st century is now a decade and a half old. Where does the United States stand? In my view, we don't have a vision for ourselves, for our role — politically, economically, militarily, and morally — in the world at the present or in the global order projecting forward. We don't have a vision for our role or identity in the Middle East, just as we don't have one for ourselves in Central Asia or Africa. We can identify the threats. We know how we've attempted to counter them. We've tried conventional warfare. We've tried counterinsurgency. We've tried (we're trying it now) counterterrorism.

What exactly are we seeking to accomplish?

What future do we hope to produce?

What is the nature of the threat or threats we're seeking to counter?

And what, if anything, works against these threats?

This book offers an answer.

Scott Mann's *Game Changers* articulates a vision for America's role in the present and future world order. It defines the threats the free world faces today and is likely to confront in the decades ahead. And it offers a strategy that, in my opinion, is not only the right one (or at least a right one, in the sense of a concept that holds out a reasonable possibility of success), but one whose implementation taps into the strongest and most honorable elements in our national character and allows us to remain true to our ideals as Americans.

Scott Mann was a lieutenant colonel in the Special Forces. He served three combat tours, not only as a fighter but, in his own phrase, "running the seams" between the upper, middle, and on-the-ground echelons of the struggle in Afghanistan. He saw what worked and what didn't. He lived with practitioners who succeeded and with others who failed.

The solution he offers is not easy. It's not a magic bullet. It can't be set up overnight, and it won't yield results, if indeed it does, in the span of one news cycle or a hundred news cycles. Further, Mann's vision does not follow conventional notions and will not be promulgated via the conventional chain of command. In many ways, it is a threat to the conventional chain of command.

Scott Mann calls this vision a game changer. Its implementation starts at the bottom, not at the top. It draws its power from indigenous elements on the ground — from "We, the people," if you will — and expands incrementally up the food chain. In tradecraft terms, it calls for what one Special Forces officer described as "warfare at the Ph.D. level." In policy terms, it demands less in blood and treasure but far more in individual and force-wide commitment, understanding, and depth of purpose.

"Bottom-up, not top-down."

"Get in and get surrounded."

"Meet them where they are."

"Tell a story that sticks."

These principles have been tried, and they work. They have worked in the real world, in the worst places that American and allied warriors have fought.

More important, in my view, the approach articulated in these pages represents a wholly original way of looking at America's role in the world and a doable program for countering the dangerous and constantly mutating threats the United States faces and will face in the future.

These "game changer" doctrines are not taught at West Point. Not yet anyway. Maybe soon. Maybe sooner than we can imagine.

— Steven Pressfield

PART I

Defining the Game

Chapter 1

Introduction

"Insanity: doing the same thing over and over again and expecting different results."

— Albert Einstein

Somewhere over southwest Asia, 2006

It had been a banner year for man hunting in Afghanistan. Over the last six months, our Green Beret Task Force had killed and captured an astounding number of Taliban leaders and fighters. I'd just completed a combat tour in the coveted Group Operations Officer billet, where I'd planned and executed missions at the most senior levels. Intelligence estimates told us we had dealt our enemy a strong blow. Our goal had been to kill as many al Qa'ida and Taliban as possible, and we did, in spades.

So as I made that long flight home from my second deployment, I should have been proud. But my heart was heavy.

Because I knew the truth. We all did.

Our victories were temporary. The Taliban would bounce back, stronger than ever. They always did. They'd lick their wounds and work even harder to co-opt a rural populace that we were almost completely ignoring.

What was worse, we should have known better. We weren't the first ones to learn these painful lessons. The history of that region, and those people, was written bold and clear.

A "Great Game" had been underway for control of that country for thousands of years. Alexander the Great, the British Empire, the Soviet Union — all had tried and failed to wrest control of that region. Those great empires eventually withdrew, defeated by a clan society that seemed primitive in comparison, yet which had withstood the best efforts, superior technology, and great finances of those larger aggressors again and again.

That was 2006.

Today, the United States and its allies are losing this Great Game for the same reasons our predecessors did. What's more, the Taliban persist for the same reasons ALL violent Islamic extremists — al Qa'ida, ISIS, and whoever succeeds them — persist.

We have not learned from history, and until we do, we will be condemned to repeat it.

As of August 2016, 6,860 American troops have been killed in the fighting in Iraq and Afghanistan — more than double the number killed on 9/11.[1] According to a study by *The New York Times*, the United States has outspent al Qa'ida approximately *seven million to one*.[2] And yet:

- Today al Qa'ida controls an unprecedented amount of territory and popular support.

- The U.S. is returning to Iraq as it teeters on the brink of chaos and ISIS (Islamic State in Iraq and Syria) domination.

- The Afghanistan government is in disarray and its security forces are incapable of sustained unilateral action in contested areas. The Taliban have regrouped and control significant parts of the country again. Al Qa'ida is already operating in multiple provinces throughout the country, and the Islamic State is also gaining a foothold there.

- ISIS has emerged as an even more powerful terror group than al Qa'ida. Our fight with these violent extremists is becoming circular.

- Worse, violent extremist influence in the West, and even the U.S., is growing like mold in a damp outhouse.

Despite all of the blood and treasure spent to date, we are now involved on multiple fronts with violent extremists across the globe, using the same failed methods. And the enemy is far from disheartened: "We might be tired of the Global War on Terror, but the Global War on Terror is not tired of the West," says Walter Russell Mead, professor of Foreign Affairs and Humanities at Bard College.[3]

But there is a better way.

There are combat-proven, cost-effective methods to stabilize at-risk areas and render violent extremists globally irrelevant. The program outlined in this book is not theory. It works. It has been tested. And it presents a specific framework that can be employed immediately.

These best practices are based on this fundamental truth:

There are many people in rough places around the world who are willing to locally resist violent extremism, if we only give them the tools and the incentive.

This is not only a war of attrition, it is a war of narratives. How can you defeat a group, when each time you kill one member, you create another, and also reinforce a new generation's hatred of you? You can't.

Defeating violent extremists means more than man hunting — it means rendering them irrelevant in the eyes of the societies they depend upon for safe haven. Losing their safe haven leaves them globally impotent and decimates their ability to project violence and realize their dream of an Islamic Caliphate.

Game Changers proposes *a local, bottom-up stabilization approach*, which is a paradigm shift from how we operate today. Many of the recommendations go against the grain of conventional counterinsurgency. That is precisely the point.

Specifically, it involves initiatives like:

- Flat decision making

- Collaboration on problem framing

- Relationships over transactions

- Surgical lethality (which is subservient to broader stability)

- Longer time horizons

- Smaller operational footprints

- Human connections and empathy, and

- Most importantly, going local to achieve relative stability.

We know this approach works because it was tried and was succeeding, until it was over-loved and killed by our senior leaders before it could take root.

We will explore what went wrong the first time, how we can avoid those errors again.

THE KEY: VILLAGE STABILITY OPERATIONS

In January 2010, during my third and final combat tour in Afghanistan, I became involved in a program known as Village Stability Operations (VSO). This was a local approach to defeating violent extremists implemented late in the war. It quickly had dramatic effects at all levels.

As the VSO Team Lead for all of U.S. Special Operations Command, my job was to help implement the program in new areas of Afghanistan, build strategic support for it at home and abroad, and share best practices with all relevant parties. I led the overall training and preparation for any units who would conduct or support VSO in Afghanistan. I have been involved with this local approach from its earliest stages. I also drafted the first-ever VSO methodology, which ultimately became the standard approach for all Special Operations Forces (SOF) in Afghanistan.

To be clear, while I have been referred to as the "Father of VSO" or the "Architect of VSO," that is not accurate. Many deserve this title, but not me. The truth is, I care more about solutions and passing on knowledge and perspective than titles or credit. And as someone who has spent more time studying and practicing this approach than anyone I know of, I believe I can provide that. I am deeply grateful to all of those whose hard work has preceded this work.

Over two years of research went into this effort. My body of research includes a wide range of academic sources, my life experience as a U.S. Army Green Beret, and also many personal interviews at formal and informal levels of civil society. Since we started the Village Stability program, I have interviewed over 5,500 special operators, conventional warriors, diplomats, development experts, nonprofit organizations, Afghan government officials, and tribal elders.

Let me share a secret: going local scared the hell out of al Qa'ida and the Taliban. Its cousin, known as the "Sons of Iraq" program, decimated the early beginnings of ISIS in Iraq. It rallied rural villages that had long since caved under extremist domination. It brought interagency and multinational parties to a level of collaboration never before seen in the entire 14-year Afghan campaign. Yes, there were challenges with going local, which we will explore. But there's much more that can be learned and used again.

I know firsthand that this approach works.

The question is: Do we have the patience and will to victory that it requires?

Chapter 2

Why We Are Losing

The book *A Practical Course for Guerilla War* by Abd al-Aziz al-Moqrin explains the ultimate goal of al Qa'ida, ISIS, and other Islamic extremist groups: "A pure Islamic system free from defects and infidel elements."[1] Senior terror analyst Jimmie Youngblood states it even more simply: "The stated al Qa'ida objective is a Pan-Islamic Caliphate."

The original Islamic Caliphate was formed after the death of the Prophet Muhammad in 632 C.E. under four central rulers, or caliphs. It included a massive expanse of land that included southwest Asia, North Africa, and Spain.[2] This is what the extremists want: the destruction of existing states in that region and the acquisition of massive amounts of territory, run according to their fundamentalist interpretation of the Koran — a religious state that suppresses democracy, subjugates women as virtual slaves, and uses brutal violence in enforcing its laws.

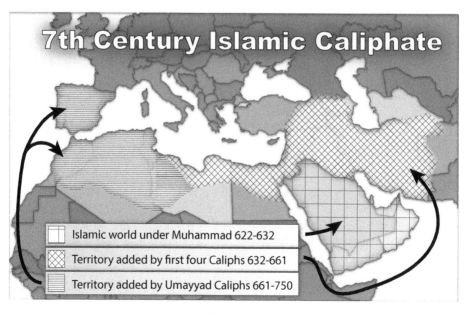

Figure 2-1
Islamic Caliphate

It has been easy for us to underestimate Islamist extremists — easy to make assumptions about their abilities from their relative lack of material wealth and possessions when compared to the Western world. However, theirs strengths and aptitudes are many. They are historically and culturally astute, highly motivated and ideologically committed, and adept at selling their narrative.

Most importantly, they currently are stronger in two fundamental areas than we are: the patience to pursue their goals over years, through significant setbacks, and across changes in leadership; and the unwavering will to WIN.

The will to win

"How can you say we don't want to win?" you might ask. "After over 15 years of war and thousands of dead?" My answer to that is this: *There is a big difference between not wanting to lose and a commitment to win.*

Not wanting to lose looks like this:

- One administration undoing the foreign policy and national security programs of the last;

- Pursuing short-term objectives to satisfy the limited patience and attention span of the public instead of long-term strategy;

- Internal bipartisan infighting;

- Retreating into a regressive fantasy of American isolationism;

- Mitigating political risk by conducting war through drone strikes from 30,000 feet.

Wanting to win looks like this:

- Commitment to a long-term program that remains consistent across party lines and multiple administrations;

- Understanding and respecting the differences in culture, psychology, and social structure in that part of the world, while exploiting enemy vulnerabilities for the defeat of the extremists;

- Recognizing that our most powerful asset against the forces of tyranny is the inherent human desire to live free. The vast majority of Muslims in the world want the same thing every person does — safety, security from terror and violence, and the freedom to live their lives.

Violent Islamist extremists, like any other enemy the U.S. has faced, can be defeated. But in a Western world of attention deficit and instant gratification, we must embrace a more powerful will to win. We must accept that the necessary actions will transcend politics-as-usual and take time to succeed.

If we can strengthen our resolve and lose the desire for immediate impact, *Game Changers* can show how to prepare ourselves smartly, efficiently, and effectively for the determined campaign we must undertake with both our soft and hard power.

> *"If you know the enemy and know yourself, you need not fear the result of a hundred battles. If you know yourself but not the enemy, for every victory gained you will also suffer a defeat. If you know neither the enemy nor yourself, you will succumb in every battle."*

> — Sun Tzu, *The Art of War*

We have ignored the violent extremists' center of gravity

Let's not ignore the truth: our failures have been bipartisan. Both the Bush and Obama administrations made errors in the War on Terror.

After toppling the Taliban and Saddam Hussein's regime, rather than focusing on *rural instability* and *local traditional governance*, the Bush administration focused on increasing the stability and power of the *formal government*. This approach ignored the differences in how our societies operate. It assumed that policing, military action, and a token amount of support and development would create long-term order. Not so.

In Afghanistan, the Bush administration propped up and promoted a corrupt, unrepresentative government. They filled the government with the very warlords who had preyed on the Afghan people for years! Before coalition forces arrived in 2001–02, these predatory leaders were so harsh on local Afghans that people initially welcomed the brutal arrival of the Taliban in the mid 1990s as a relief from warlord oppression.

The Obama administration likewise dropped the ball. They killed Bin Laden, which had a significant effect on violent extremism. Then, however, they set a timetable for withdrawal that ignored the critical need for continued development and support in the fragile Iraqi and Afghan states.

People were tired of the war, and instead of telling them the hard truth that continued, long-term action was necessary, the administration declared mission accomplished and began pulling out before the governments were strong enough to handle their own factions, infighting, and extremists.

The results have been clear: almost daily suicide bombings in both countries, the loss of massive territory to the Taliban, and the shockingly fast rise of ISIS as an organized and powerful threat across the world, even in our own country.

The reason these approaches fail is *because the real center of gravity in these cultures is local clan populations.* The clans, not the government, are the source of the fighters, resources, money, and ideas. The populations have been betrayed and let down by their governments for so many generations, there is no trust left at all — especially for a government propped up by a foreign power perceived as hostile. And yet these inept and corrupt "partners" are the exact parties through which the State Department, U.S. Agency for International Development (USAID), and Defense Department project our influence.

We think top-down, rather than bottom-up

Dr. Phil Williams is an expert on the role of alternative governance and its impact on the emergence of transnational crime. "Less than 25 percent of the countries around the world are considered strong governments," he said in a recent lecture. These formal governments are known as 'top-down.' "But, despite this shortfall in governments, our only intervention approach is always top-down."[3]

The overreliance on partner governments, no matter how inept or corrupt, is one of the major reasons we're losing this game. Our model of traditional statecraft and counterinsurgency is the wrong model for dealing with a threat that thrives in hard-to-reach places. Unfortunately, it is all we know.

We must learn to value the informal systems of society that locals value, because they offer the most viable platforms for stability. We must discover who the local people, not we, define as the legitimate leaders of an area, even if they are from less formal structures than we are used to dealing with.

Extremists exploit fear and want by offering meaning to their strug-gle. When people are poor and desperate, they are vulnerable to hate and extremism. These people care about whether they have water, or what tribes are at war with them, not our rhetoric or our short-term charity that evaporates when we pull out.

We also ignore the resilient indigenous leaders, often in the shad-ows, who can offer solutions to these festering local problems. When we ignore what the populations really need and care about, we make ourselves irrelevant. Without relevance, we struggle to find a credible narrative that paints us as anything other than enemies.

Working from the top-down ignores local realities and transforms us into occupiers. And now, as we return to Iraq, we begin to repeat our mistakes. We ignore the Sunni tribes and other minority groups and focus almost exclusively on the Shia-dominated government. Instead of reaching out to the Sunni tribal leaders who resisted al Qa'ida in the Awakening of the Iraqi surge, we now try to disrupt ISIS with air strikes into these same tribal areas.

Violent extremists control their safe havens

To be effective, violent extremists need room to plan, train, inspire, proj-ect, and control operations without outside intervention. They do this in areas known as safe havens or sanctuaries. They live among the neigh-borhoods, slums, and villages. The events of 2001 that rocked the entire world were planned in such hidden places. Extremists are very hard to target because of how they burrow into communities. They are like ticks dug into the fur of a dog, and scratching them with a big paw only makes them burrow deeper.

Extremists require weak central governments and terrain where the government can't or won't reach. These undergoverned areas are nor-mally dominated by clans and tribes exerting power in the absence of the government. It is an honor-based culture where hospitality, revenge, and feud are the order of the day. And after all these years, we still know very little about these cultures.

Many of these areas don't like outsiders, whether they are U.S. forces or violent extremists. Local communities *will* try to fight back against extremist control. But communities that once handled their own form of local security now can't protect their own villages. They're poor and suffering. Worse, the social structure has broken down: pragmatic traditional leaders, who once regulated disputes between feuding clans,

11

now are in disarray. This absence of order allows honor, revenge, and feud to run rampant. Because the traditional structures are frayed or broken, the locals find it very difficult to stand up against the extremists for too long.

Because of the chaos, poverty, and extremists, inhabitants are leaving many rural areas. As detailed in David Kilcullen's outstanding 2013 book, *Out of the Mountains*, the extremists are beginning to move with them into new forms of urban safe haven, to which we have yet to adapt.[4]

Unfortunately, rather than taking advantage of the natural local resistance to extremist control, we would rather disrupt their safe havens than deny them altogether. When we rely more on drone strikes and night raids than persistent presence at local levels, it has a double negative effect: it creates only a temporary disruption in operations, while fueling tribal anger against us.

Worse yet, we're not even always on the right battlefield — we prefer to operate in capital cities and major trade corridors, not the small villages and crowded shantytowns that are the true epicenters of safe haven. When we do construct remote outposts, they look like a modern-day 'Fort Apache,' replete with 20-foot concrete blast barriers and concertina wire. They are hardly 'population-centric' as our Counterinsurgency (COIN) doctrine proclaims. On rare occasions, when resources actually make it to potential safe haven communities, they hardly ever redress the true needs expressed from within the communities.

Violent extremists understand that all politics are local. They act locally, and then project globally. They both support and terrorize local populations, depending on the individual vulnerabilities of the area. Their methods for moving into communities range from beheadings and public beatings to winning loyalty by providing economic development or security against predatory government security forces.

Luckily, they are not always as smart as they should be: many extremists don't always value local realties. Many of them demonstrate complete disdain toward traditional clan society and openly disrespect tribal culture. These missteps are what create many of the game-changing opportunities I present throughout this book. But the window of opportunity is closing as these extremists continue to learn.

One thing is certain: Whether through coercion or persuasion, violent extremists build local presence and credibility before they project their global reach. This local approach, no matter which side does it, is very effective.

Also certain is the fact that in these rough places, our strategy of using government control as the singular means for stability is a fool's errand.

Violent extremists have a better narrative than we do

Islamic extremists mobilize their followers through master narratives pulled from the ashes of conflict that connect to their history and culture. They reach deep into the emotions of Muslims to create a burning desire to re-establish Islam's rightful place in the world.

In addition to having a master narrative that rings true with their followers, they also tell excellent stories through a variety of mediums. They are masters at digital and social media and don't have cumbersome communications procedures to release their story. ISIS, for example, beheads people on YouTube and their Al Hayat media company garners a global following in the process.

Additionally, their local presence allows them to fit the story to the audience in everyday conversations in local communities. This shapes ideology and fuels their support in more and more areas like Syria, Indonesia, and even the Philippines.

Because we have no persistent presence locally, violent extremists tell our story for us. It's easy to show Islam under attack by the U.S. if you are an extremist living among the locals. All they must do is point to our myriad drone strikes, collateral damage of innocent lives, large troop deployments, or obscenely expensive development programs that only further enrich power brokers at the expense of local peasants.

The U.S., on the other hand, never established a compelling alternative narrative. Our narratives failed to influence Islamic populations, because they revealed a fundamental lack of understanding and respect for even the moderates within their populations.

Over time, as the initial outpouring of resolve after 9/11 faded, our narrative even failed to influence our own citizens. We let the precious resource of support ebb away, one yellow ribbon at a time. As our liberation of Afghanistan turned into a long-term counterinsurgency campaign, Americans rightfully wondered why we were committing blood and treasure to build a government that was corrupt and didn't seem to want us there.

Even the phrase 'Global War on Terror' is ill conceived from a narrative perspective. How do you defeat 'terror'? This narrative has no resonance with the Islamic world, nor is it specific enough to craft a campaign. To the Islamic base of support known as the Ummah, our efforts to fight terror have made us the 'Boogey Man' or 'The Great Satan.' We are the manifestation of evil and the obstacle to Islamic greatness.

And we have provided no story to refute this, or behaviors to replace it.

Our internal process and structure are ineffective and too complex

We create a lot of our own challenges. Government parochialism and rivalries over roles and budgets prevent us from achieving unity of effort. The local grievances, exploited by extremists, are usually far too complex for any one person or organization to accurately frame or solve on their own. So we just ignore these problems because they are too hard.

There was a time when we could get away with our outdated organizational structure and top-down process of dealing with violent extremists. Today, this outdated approach enables violent extremists to portray us to the Islamic world as a looming threat and that locals should rise up and strike back against us.

We don't want to look at ourselves from this local perspective. The notions of identity and trust as sources of instability, longer foreign engagement timelines, and working with tribal community leaders are all less attractive and higher risk than drone strikes, making many politicians very uncomfortable. But if we want to win, we had better get used to it.

We have to learn from our mistakes.

Violent extremists are changing the game as they go

Violent extremists are usually patient and adapt based on their mistakes. Their growing understanding that they need to embrace local reality, not change it, is a prime example. They "have recognized that if the group wants to live and train in, and then attack from, and return to safe haven in someone else's territory, they cannot call the tune regarding how their hosts live, pray, and behave — but rather they must, to some extent, learn to live and behave like the locals," says renowned al Qa'ida expert and author of *Imperial Hubris*, Michael Scheuer.[5]

In a letter admonishing extremist fighters for roughing up locals in North Africa, al Qa'ida leader Abdelmalek Droukdal emphasized the need to "win public opinion" and "take the environment into consideration." He went on to write, "We should be sure to win allies, be flexible in dealing with the realities, and compromise on some rights to achieve greater interest."[6] In Afghanistan, Taliban leader Mullah Omar issued a similar manifesto of inclusion and greater tolerance from his fighters toward locals.

Violent extremists can replicate this model globally from Syria to Syracuse

The model they developed in Afghanistan — think globally, act locally — works. They have been so successful in Iraq and Afghanistan with this approach, they are now moving on to other countries such as Yemen, Mali, Syria, and Somalia. Today's violent extremist groups are immensely talented entrepreneurs of myth and violence, and they are scaling their product for global distribution into the West.

The psychological game: bait and switch

There is one more component to the game. It's the "sudden death" period before the game is over, when emotions run high and tempers flare, when desperation to "do something" in the face of audacious violence upon our own people actually leads us to uninformed, reactionary deeds.

It's the point in the game when we get sucked in even deeper by our enemies, by design.

Violent extremists *want us* to mobilize against them. They need us as their enemy. Each terror attack, every beheading, pulls us deeper into this war. And attacking us at home, where it hurts most, guarantees the pissed-off, callous enemy they crave.

Our response to these imminent attacks will be predictable. It'll be the same as happened after 9/11. A horrendous attack on America. Terrible loss of life. Disbelief, giving way to anger and the need for revenge. Tens of thousands of warriors with cropped hair and determined faces boarding aircraft to make the long flight. The media salivating and covering every moment, stoking the war fury.

This time it won't be my tired bones on that deployment aircraft. It will be my son. He wants to be a Green Beret like his Dad. Perhaps he'll be seated next to your son or daughter for the long flight over.

Our enemies will feel the military might the U.S. can bring to bear. But as we shock and awe them, they will be digging back in, letting us do precisely what they wanted. Create more hate in the populations. Bleed us to the point of bankruptcy. And worse, make us in our bloodlust ignore everything we could have learned. Instead of patience and working locally, we'll want big, fast successes for the public to digest.

As one senior flamboyant Green Beret commanding officer would bark to his men before every Special Forces pre-mission brief early in the Afghan campaign, "I don't care about anything else, just tell me how many Taliban you're going to kill."

We'll lose hundreds. We'll kill tens of thousands. It will seem like a clear victory for the far superior American military. But as time marches on, we will wonder why the foreign central government we're throwing billions of dollars at can't extend influence or power beyond the capital. One by one, the American flags will come off the porches as flag-draped caskets come home. The patriotic songs will fade and our collective lust for vengeance will weaken under the weight of an Islamist narrative that rallies wannabe jihadists the world over to their enduring cause.

Before we realize what has happened, our celebrated liberation will become an unwelcome occupation. The goal of establishing the Islamic Caliphate will be one step closer.

Just the way they planned it.

Looking forward by looking back

As I made that flight home from my second Afghan combat tour, these realizations were not clear to me yet. I only knew our approach wasn't working. Now, over a decade later, as we pack up in Afghanistan and face the new threat of ISIS, it's becoming painfully obvious how this game is played, and who is winning.

While every area in the world is different, our Afghan experience gives us knowledge and self-clarity like never before. In fact, it's the foundation and context for changing the game.

To do this, we must set aside — if only for now — the desire to forget Afghanistan. We must learn its lessons properly, or else continue to lose by our own hand.

Chapter Highlights

- *Violent extremists want to return to the former glory of an Islamic Caliphate.*

- *Instead of defeating violent Islamist extremists, we are trying not to lose. This middle-of-the-road political approach weakens our country and empowers our enemy.*

- *U.S. foreign policy and strategy fail to engage extremists within their own center of gravity — local aggrieved populations. It reinforces the extremists' advantage by concentrating only on forcing distrusted foreign government authority on local people.*

- *Our ineffective structure and process are no longer just a waste of blood and treasure — they fuel the extremist narrative that "the U.S. is attacking Islam," and put our country at deeper risk for attack.*

- *Violent extremists are beating us in the war of narratives.*

- *Violent extremists have a model for expansion that worked well in Afghanistan and they are now expanding to Syria, Iraq, and other areas.*

- *Violent extremists are drawn to violent tribal or clan areas where they supplant traditional systems with their own brand of governance.*

- *Violent extremists establish safe haven to project against the U.S. and "near Satan" apostate governments.*

- *When we target those safe haven areas from the top down, the violent extremists burrow into the population — and we lose even more credibility with their hosts.*

- *We are being baited. Our emotional post–9/11 reaction is exactly what violent extremists want us to do again and again to mobilize their religious population base in the war against the West.*

Chapter 3

Where the Pavement Ends

Introduction to the graveyard

As we made the final turn for our approach into the Afghan army compound, I saw for the first time the real graveyard of empires.

It was 2004, during my first combat tour in Afghanistan. My Special Forces battalion was headquartered at Kandahar Airfield, responsible for Special Operations activities in the southern and western parts of Afghanistan.

As my sergeant major and I drove around Kandahar to familiarize ourselves, we detoured to the local Afghan Army base. We wanted to see where the Afghan National Army (ANA), our new partners for future combat operations, lived.

To get there, we had to drive through a large former Soviet Union base. In the 1980s, it had been a sprawling housing area for Soviet officers and senior NCOs, full of single-story structures with carports and symmetrical yards and gardens. No more.

Everything was dilapidated and caving in. As we saw the debris-filled swimming pool, the mechanical boneyard full of rusted war machines, I did not realize I might be seeing a premonition of our own future.

Entire Soviet armored divisions had gone up against traditional tribal society and lost. The traditional governance structure of village elders, known as the *jirga*, proved to be a more resilient form of Afghan governance than anything the Kremlin and the Afghan Communists could muster.

My Dad, a Civil War buff, would take my brother and me to battlefields in the southern U.S. when we were young. With his help, we were able to discern clear insights from the historical details of the fights on a local, personal level. We learned just how much wisdom could be extracted by studying the actions of these historic battles.

But here, even though every rotting tank and personnel carrier had its own tragic story to tell, the battles were too fresh. I could not make their lessons out, other than a voice on the hot desert wind that warned that there was still plenty of room in this boneyard.

As my normally talkative sergeant major and I drove in silence, it occurred to me that our equipment, our sprawling base, our Burger Kings and other soldier comfort stores — a mere stone's throw away from here — looked a lot like this place.

These rusted hulks and collapsed buildings were a dull reminder of the lack of understanding the Soviet Union and the U.S. have had for the real Afghanistan. They never realized that beyond this façade of modernity, beyond the protective wire and armed sentries, the pavement came to an abrupt end.

And where the pavement ends, the real Afghanistan begins.

Where the pavement ends

The inability of Afghan society to solve its own social grievances, the increased distrust between outlying Afghan communities and the Afghan government, and our uninformed actions as a coalition set the stage for the most sinister component of the violent extremist threat model we are seeing around the world today — extremist exploitation of local communities.

Afghanistan is one of the most rural, primitive and poverty-stricken countries in the world. Over 75 percent of Afghanistan's 30 million people still live in rural villages.[1] Less than one in three Afghans has electrical power.[2] It is primarily an agriculture-based society and less than 12 percent of the land is arable.[3]

Kabul, Afghanistan's capital city, along with regional urban centers in Kandahar and Jalalabaad, look much more like the Western world. Formal government, rule of law, and armed security forces answer to the state in a structured way. No wonder these urban places were the areas where the Soviets and NATO decided to set up their headquarters and focus their counterinsurgency efforts. You gravitate to what is familiar.

But in Afghanistan, there are two completely different worlds, two sets of culture and values. Peering out from the relative comfort of a forward operating base or down from a helicopter skimming the desert terrain, the mud huts and walled compounds of Afghanistan's rural villages look more like desert mirages from a *Star Wars* movie than functioning, dynamic communities. But those outlying areas are real.[4] They lay beyond the reach of the Afghan government. They have their own local realities, which comprise a type of civil society very different from what we know and understand.

Radically different from the NATO and Kabul norms of formal civil society, these principles of rural, informal civil society define the collective identity of the primary areas of the Afghan. Understanding how Afghan societies handle their business provides excellent context for understanding other status societies around the globe at risk for violent extremist exploitation.

Gap between top and bottom

"Afghanistan is a country defined by social mobilizations and uprisings," explained Dr. Seth Jones, one of the architects of VSO, to a group of Navy SEALS, Green Berets, and Marines preparing for deployment to Afghanistan.

Stability in Afghanistan has been shaky in the best of times. Even during the so-called Afghan "Golden Era" of the 1920s through the 1970s, there was a distinct gap between the government and its largely rural population. Stability never approached anything we would accept in our modern context of a liberal democracy, which puts the rights of the individual above the extended family, group, or clan.[5]

The central government has never really controlled the vast Afghan lands. There was always a shaky balance during periods of relative stability that often fell prey to social uprisings and mass violence.

State Department veteran Casey Johnson, as a governance advisor in Kandahar Province, was a new, yet rare breed of civilian stability advisor who both understood the formal elements of state diplomacy and clan society's relevance to overall stability. In dissecting how the government before 1978 worked, he concluded: "The government never went down into the villages unless requested; it strayed no further than the district level and let local leaders — in some areas tribal elders and in others religious figures — make decisions for their villages. In return for this autonomy the villages remained loyal to the state."[6]

Dr. Ted Callahan, one of the most knowledgeable Westerners I have ever met regarding Afghanistan and its culture, concurred. "Throughout Afghanistan's turbulent history, the only service provided by the Afghan state to the outlying areas was security," he explained to me in one of our many mentoring sessions. "Today they can't even provide that."[7]

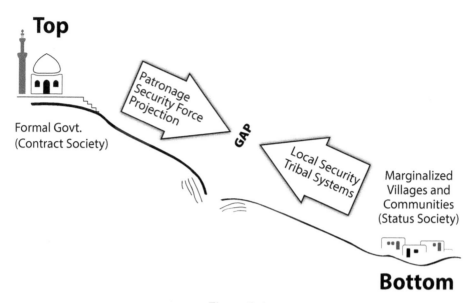

Figure 3-1
Afghan Relative Stability, 1920s–1970s
Stability during this time was relative to the relationship
between contract and status society.

In his book *Jirgas*, Dr. Khan Idris, a Pashtun tribesman from eastern Afghanistan, describes his government's involvement in rural affairs as something that only occurred when local violence reached unacceptable levels. When absolutely necessary, Afghan security forces would launch into rural areas, thump heads, and fall back to their urban bases.

Dr. Thomas Barfield, author of *Afghanistan, a Political and Cultural History*, did much to shape Special Operations' understanding of the value of Afghanistan's informal clan society. "In rural Afghanistan, where the majority of the population resides, local populations expect, where possible, to solve their own problems through mediation and arbitration conducted by people of their own choosing."[8]

Previous Afghan leaders who understood this reality held the secret to the stability puzzle we were trying to solve. They knew that in exchange for letting the local communities solve their own problems and make their own decisions, the locals would in turn "recognize the sovereignty of the Afghan national state" and not challenge its legitimacy.

Despite this local empowerment, however, there was always a trust gap between the government and the outlying communities.

The gap with Pashtun tribes

This trust gap was especially prevalent in the Pashtun-dominated areas of eastern and southern Afghanistan, as well as the isolated enclaves of Pashtuns in the west and north. The Pashtuns were the most tribal, violent, and austere ethnic group in the country. Pashtun tribal areas were the source of historical uprisings and are still the heart of the Afghan insurgency.

One Afghan agricultural report states that a major reason for the lack of Afghan government legitimacy is the significant disconnect between the conservative, traditional rural Afghan populations and the urban populations. The rural communities perceive the urbanites as arrogant and disrespectful of traditional values and customs. They resent the fact that the "young city boys look down on elders and think they know everything" and "they [the urbanites] are ashamed of being a member of a tribe, they are ashamed of being Pashtu — they are not welcome here."

Where the pavement ends in Afghanistan, clans and tribes rule. "The rural populations, with their tribal structures, control Southern Afghanistan," the report explains. "The rural populations are the center of gravity in this counterinsurgency, and they know it."[9]

Clash of clans

Why do Pashtuns and other areas of rural Afghanistan push back against the government? As Randall McCoy, in the History Channel miniseries *Hatfields and McCoys*, said: "It's about honor." Honor in societies plays a much bigger stability role than we realize. This is true from Scots-Irish clans, where I hail from in Appalachia, to the Pashtun tribes of Afghanistan and Pakistan.

Dr. Mark Weiner is an award-winning law professor and author whose work on clans is essential to changing the game against violent extremists. In his book *The Rule of the Clan*, Dr. Weiner highlights two very different societies that are clashing more and more these days:

First are the traditional, honor-based *Societies of Status*. We can define these status societies as traditional, informal or clan societies. They mandate loyalty to a group and willingness to fight to defend the honor of the group above all.

Then there are *Societies of Contract*. We can define them as "formal" society. They emphasize the individual and rule of law. These are our

Western societies as well as other urban areas in Afghanistan, such as Kabul.[10]

Many of our challenges since September 11, 2001 stem from our failure to grasp the fundamental differences between status societies and contract societies. The biases we project can be destructive, if we simply view Westerners as "civilized" and clan societies as savages. It is a simplistic view that ignores the important differences that are critical to winning the war.

In societies of status, *the clan* is at the center of daily life. In societies of contract, the *individual* is at the heart of all we do. So you can see that George W. Bush spreading democracy to the Middle East, emphasizing individual rights over the group, is not only a foreign concept but represents a threat to traditional clan ways of life.

Honor and *shame* are also very important in status society. "A world where a man's reputation is at the center of his livelihood and self-worth" is an honor society, writes Malcolm Gladwell in his book *Outliers*. The rules of *Pashtunwali* or "code of the Pashtun," for example, are completely based on honor. "Honor tends to be most prominent in settings where possessions are easily expropriated, overarching, political authority is weak, and reputations are well known."[11] This means that one's honor is literally tied to survival and to the collective status of one's group. Defending honor is a requirement of clan society.

At one end of the honor spectrum is *hospitality*, and on the other, *revenge*. We often overlook the significance of hospitality in clan society. It is not uncommon for a clansman to invite you into his home and share his last good quarter of meat with you. He does this to preserve his honor with his clan.

In contrast, drone strikes, night raids into Afghan homes, and other combat operations often flew in the face of clan hospitality. This led to revenge attacks due to perceived loss of honor. Many of the insurgent actions, improvised explosive attacks, and insider threat attacks on coalition forces by Afghan security forces actually had less to do with ideology than with perceived honor violations.

In status society, resolving disputes in the most practical way possible is more important than objectively determining fault. When honor is at stake, revenge is often expected. Revenge often escalates into feud. These clan conflicts can escalate into unmanageable blood feuds. Left unchecked, feuds can last generations and result in massive casualties on both sides. Even genocide can occur.

Therefore, dispute resolution, which usually involves various forms of atonement and restoring relationships, is a critical component of status society. Status society leaders have always kept things on an even keel. Establishing and maintaining relationships are important to every aspect of status society. When it comes to feud, whether it's a simple public apology or submitting several head of livestock to the other party, restoring honor to strained relationships becomes tantamount to local stability.

Note: Understanding how atonement works at an interpersonal level, along with how disputes are solved in clan society, is vitally important and offers unique opportunities for advisors and practitioners who go local.

Local autonomy

Pashtuns are the epitome of the clan society, the largest tribal group in the world, comprising almost 50 percent of the Afghan population. With only a few exceptions, Pashtun monarchs have ruled Afghanistan. Yet, because of their clannish nature, Pashtuns have also always been very distrustful of the Afghan government. They operated with autonomy. Pashtun kings used patronage and state violence to keep the tribal chiefs in check. Other than that, locals handled their own affairs.

This clan and feudal form of civil society was much different than the formal institutions of the U.S., or even the Kabul monarchy. The Pashtun tribal areas historically functioned with a code of honor and shame known as Pashtunwali.

Violence, tied to honor, is a common occurrence in Pashtun tribal areas. There is a saying: 'Me against my brother; my brother and me against my cousin; my brother, my cousin and me against the world.' Tribal rivalries are frequent in this resource-scarce environment. Shortages in arable land, food insecurity, and inheritance issues are but a few of the local issues that can lead to group tension.

Conflicts were resolved through an informal governance system known as the jirga. This council of local elders consisted of established family leaders. Jirgas used restorative justice to resolve feuds. They maintained societal balance rather than imposing rigid rules of law. By repairing relationships and maintaining group honor, jirgas kept things on an even keel. This balance, essential to the Afghan state for stability, the Afghan government could not provide.

Another essential factor to local stability was security. Once, local, community-based security was common in these rural Pashtun areas. Small village-based security groups were accountable to the jirga and enforced its decisions. Most were farmers, but like the militia volunteers of colonial America, they could quickly assemble and defend their communities in the event of attack. They were often referred to as *Arbakai*. This community security they provided was extremely effective and very legitimate in local eyes.

Another locally handled area of stability was *economic development*. Under the leadership of elders, rural Afghans would do communal work for their village and farms,[12] such as cleaning waterways and canals before the planting season.[13] To fund these projects, elders would impose taxes locally as required.[14]

The robust capacity of Pashtun tribal society to handle most of its day-to-day affairs resulted in minimal reliance on the Afghan government. Pashtun tribal society played a critical role in the uneasy balance of status and contract society from the 1920s through most of the 1970s.

This relative stability would change forever when the Soviet Union invaded Afghanistan in 1979.

The end of 'old school' governance

Today, Afghan clan society institutions are broken.

"The old ways of resolving conflict are gone. Elders are dead or scattered. Many of the younger generation don't respect the elders that remain. They beat them and attack them," lamented one Afghan tribal leader as we sat under the shade of a big mulberry tree to escape the oppressive Kandahar sun.[15]

The Soviets systematically dismantled clan society by targeting villages and tribes as the center of gravity. They attacked the rural power base, killing over a million Afghans, many of whom were elders (Khans). They also displaced seven million Afghans to Pakistan, and redistributed land from traditional Khans to minority tribes who had aligned with the Soviets.[16]

The religious class exploited the degradation of traditional tribe structure. There had always been an underlying tension between tribal Khans and mullahs in many rural areas. According to the International Crisis Group, the dynamic that had kept the clergy politically subordinate to tribal leadership collapsed during the jihad. "In the absence of tribal authority, madrassa-based *ulemma* (clergy), aided by Pakistan, Saudi Arabia, and the U.S. gradually filled the social and political vacuum during the Soviet jihad."[17]

The Soviet Union started a cycle of violence in Afghanistan that continued for over three decades and severely damaged the status society. This damage to clan society isn't unique to Afghanistan: while it isn't always caused by external warfare, degraded status society is a growing problem in many extremist-exploited areas around the world.

Today, there are entire villages without elder leadership. Missing are the traditional resilient leaders who were capable of maintaining a pragmatic connection between the government and local tribes. Governance, security, and economic development all suffer without traditional leadership.

The institutional know-how for day-to-day life in Afghan status society was also degraded. Even basic agricultural skills such as crop rotation, food preservation, land management, grazing practices, watershed functions, and animal husbandry were lost due to the removal of the

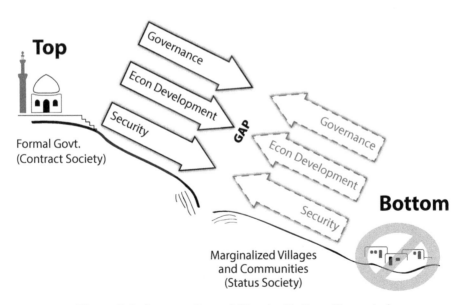

Figure 3-2 Community and Clan Institutions Degraded
Beginning with the Soviet invasion, status society began to erode
and with it, overall Afghan relative stability.

Khans.[18] Local security groups, usually accountable to the jirga, fell away and gave way to a new group of local leaders — warlords.

By the 1990s, the traditional role of elders and the respect they commanded gave way to the rise of ambitious mullahs, frustrated youth, narco-traffickers, and a range of armed thugs. This rapid decay of traditional civil society initiated by the Soviets greatly contributed to an all-out ethnic civil war.[19]

The Afghan civil war left an indelible impression of predation in the minds of millions of Afghans. The persistent black cloud of violence created hopelessness and loss of trust across the land. It is manifest today in the population's distrust of armed groups and their own government, and their deep-seated fear of another civil war.

Local exploitation for strategic gain

Starting late in 2002, Taliban insurgents started coming back into Afghan villages throughout the rural Pashtun areas of eastern and southern Afghanistan. They also infiltrated large Pashtun areas of western Afghanistan, and even some of the Pashtun enclaves in northern Afghanistan. By operating at the village level, the Taliban and other violent extremists mobilized and co-opted entire villages to support them.[20]

By going local first, they built solid rural platforms from which they could project effectively into Afghan urban areas.

By working from the bottom up, the Taliban identified and addressed grievances affecting rural Pashtun populations. In this heavily resource-scarce environment, the most commonly exploited grievance was dispute resolution. Religious Taliban *Sharia* courts, rather than the government or jirga, speedily resolved issues related to conflicts over land rights, water, and other disputes.

"The Taliban provide a service the people want...justice," Ashraf D. (that's what I'll call him) explained to me over a strong cup of Afghan chai tea. Ashraf is a tribal leader and cultural advisor to coalition forces. "They bring both parties in and usually make a decision in five to ten days. The people may not like the outcome, but they are happy to have a decision."[21]

Quick decisions by the Taliban, coupled with their ability to enforce the decision, ensure unmatched local legitimacy. These local actions add up to create social relevance, which ultimately leads to trust and

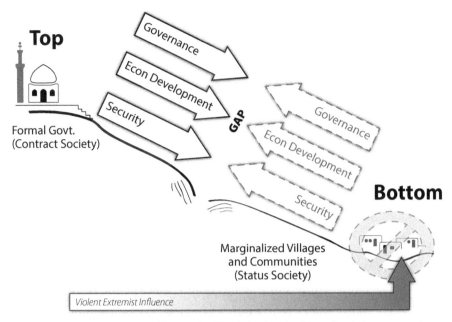

Figure 2-3 Extremist Exploitation in Clan Society
Violent extremists exploit weaknesses in status society and
replace them with their brand of local control.

local support. This is how extremists exploit the degraded traditional systems of status society and acquire strategic safe haven.

By the end of 2009, the coalition was still struggling to maintain presence on the outskirts of only a few Afghan villages, while the Taliban were at the gates of Kabul and Kandahar. They struck from rural villages at will. Going local worked like a charm for violent extremists after the coalition invaded Afghanistan.

Even where clan society structures are strong, violent extremists have learned how to degrade them. They identify and address community grievances to achieve local relevance so they can embed in these communities. This lets them project and inspire violence globally with strategic reach, cocooned in the warmth of the status society safety net.

This threat model of exploiting grievances is now playing out all over the world.

Now that we know what it looks like where the pavement ends, let's return to the Afghan graveyard and figure out what went wrong by doing that most uncomfortable of tasks...looking at ourselves.

Chapter Highlights

- *If we understand Afghan realities, we have a framework for understanding other violent extremist threat areas around the world and in our own backyard.*

- *Almost 80 percent of Afghanistan is 'off the pavement,' beyond the reach of the government.*

- *There has always been a trust gap between contract society (top) and status society (bottom).*

- *There are major differences between Afghan status society and contract society that should inform our stability actions.*

- *Afghan status society handled its own affairs until the Soviet occupation. Now it has lost much of the ability to do that.*

- *Violent extremists have co-opted vulnerable status society as safe haven and manipulated simmering notions of honor and revenge to project violence.*

- *Extremist exploitation of these vulnerable areas is happening all over the world.*

Chapter 4

Square Tank in a Round Jirga

"To impose a political system from the outside that does not correspond to local political realities is to create an artificial state, and to fail at nation building."

— John C. Hulsman, *To Begin the World Over Again*

Kandahar Province, 2010

I saw the dust from the convoy well before I saw the actual vehicles. It looked as if a massive sandstorm was approaching from the south. The only thing that indicated otherwise was the low grumble of truck engines fighting the heat and terrain.

I was standing in the courtyard of a local elder's home in Kandahar Province with a small Special Forces team. All conversation ceased as the sandstorm resolved itself into six vehicles that looked like something out of a *Mad Max* movie.

Bristling with machine guns, encased in thick armor, their simple narrative was: "Don't mess with us." As they drove past homes made of mud and camel hair, the soldiers in their turrets looked down from behind their sleek helmets, mirrored sunglasses and bulging body armor.

In this place, they looked totally alien.

I shifted my glance to the Afghan villagers I had been talking with. Some had fled into their homes at the sight of these vehicles. Children cowered behind mud walls and mulberry trees. Some of the younger men glared in simmering anger. The elder I had been meeting just shook his head sadly from side to side.

It was in that moment I knew we were losing this war.

Right war, wrong direction

By the time my second Afghan tour of duty was complete in 2006, it was clear the coalition campaign was unsuccessful. Despite high attrition against Taliban and other extremists, their reach and influence was ever expanding, while the coalition was seen more and more as an occupier rather than liberator.

The Afghan campaign started from the right direction — the bottom. The unconventional warfare utilized by Special Operations Forces shortly after September 11th, 2001 was very decisive. This approach embedded Green Berets with various ethnic clans and mobilized them to evict al Qa'ida and the Taliban from the country. This grass-roots movement emanating from status society created a lot of strategic momentum among Afghans, and even some hope. The stage was set for a small-footprint campaign to help build Afghan security capacity and foster local stability.

Most Afghans, we would learn much later, were actually ready for a community-level, long-term effort geared toward helping rural Afghanistan restore its resiliency and keeping violent extremists on the other side of the border.

"There was huge hope for the government," comments one resident of Helmand province in *Decoding the New Taliban.* "People waited for three or four years, but nothing happened. Instead the cruel leaders were redeployed and supported by the government. They brought back the jihadi leaders. We thought King Zahir Shah would return and the people would be educated and prosperous."[1]

Tragically, the Bush administration had little interest in nation building. It instead focused on hunting down extremist remnants, and tens of thousands of conventional forces military poured into Afghanistan like the spring floods coming down from the Hindu Kush. This large coalition force pursued Counterinsurgency (COIN) as its method for achieving stability — and it failed.

We were all in such a rush to get into Afghanistan that we didn't take the time to really try to understand it. Our ignorance of clan society and government corruption and incompetence prevailed through most of the Afghan campaign. It unfortunately still holds true in our engagements around the world.

Pissed off and drawn in

In fairness, it's easy to sit back now and coolly analyze things. At the time, we'd just lost 3,000 of our own people, many of them practically vaporized into the rubble at Ground Zero. We were pissed, and we wanted payback. Even Green Berets, who normally thrive on an indigenous approach, were more interested into putting bullets through al Qa'ida and the Taliban than working with the local population.

A top-down approach in a bottom-up country

As more and more conventional coalition forces flowed into Afghanistan, former Soviet bases began to swell to capacity. Military policemen put up speed limit signs. A Harley Davidson dealership for the troops even came to Bagram Air Force Base.

Beyond the pavement, in status society, those ominous-looking armored convoys flooded the tattered Afghan landscape of valleys and farms. From the capital and these large bases, the coalition began projecting security, economic development, and governance from the central government down to the rural villages — the top-down approach.

Coalition contract society, entirely alien to these people, had arrived in the graveyard of empires.

Scalps on the barn

Blinded by Western bias, we imposed a government model that was perceived by Afghans as a direct threat to their way of life. "Every occupying power tends to create a system that requires them to deal with as few locals as possible. And that's exactly what we did here," Dr. Ted Callahan, anthropologist and longtime student of northern Afghanistan, told me in an interview.[2]

The theory behind our top-down counterinsurgency was to give space for the Afghan government to grow outward from Kabul. In reality, what it did was reinforce the predatory and exploitive way the Afghan government had always dealt with its rural populations, while widening the already strained trust gap between contract and status society.

The Afghan campaign evolved into an obscenely large military endeavor, involving a large-scale but limited campaign of conventional forces, and Special Operations Forces acting like conventional forces. Despite the seemingly obvious lessons from Vietnam, body count became trendy again. Enemy attrition was a critical measure of success.[3] We briefed excited visiting Congressmen and other U.S.–based senior military leaders on numbers of Taliban killed, using PowerPoint, drone videos, and Excel spreadsheets. The phrase 'scalps on the barn' became common language throughout Afghanistan.

33

Oh, we made token efforts at 'population-centric' stability. But most of our counterinsurgency forces operated from built-up bases that provided only daylight presence in rural areas. When coalition forces returned to their bases at nightfall, the extremists jerked anyone who had supported the coalition out of their homes and beat them in front of their families. Nightfall was when children were taken. And when 'night letters' were dropped at village mosques warning of more intimidation to come if folks cooperated with us.

When we did act at night, it was often to conduct raids to interdict extremist leaders. These often unintentionally invoked Pashtun honor-based revenge, known as *badal*, by infringing on the honor of a man's home and family at night. "If someone is handcuffed in front of women, he would see no other way left, but to head toward the mountains [to fight with the insurgents]. Each night raid reinforces these perceptions and gives fresh fodder to insurgent propaganda," states the Liaison Office in a 2010 report on Afghan night raids.[4]

It wasn't just conventional forces that were enemy-centric and detached from status society. With the exception of a few units, we in Special Forces were man hunting too. Despite it being our historic function, Green Berets shunned the traditional core role of 'train, advise, and assist' in favor of lethal targeting.[5]

We were willing to pay a fortune for attrition. The U.S. spent over one trillion dollars in Afghanistan and deployed over one million troops over a 13-year period.[6] According to Giustozzi, coalition forces spent between 15 and 16 million dollars for every Taliban killed in 2005, and between 7 and 8 million dollars in 2006.[7]

Despite those expensive scalps, Taliban and other extremists continued to expand their reach and influence in the first decade of the Afghan War.

Our security approach wasn't the only problem.

If you build it, they will come...and blow it up

Our process of economic development created more problems than it solved in Afghanistan. A large component of coalition counterinsurgency efforts, projects such as schools, wells, and paved roads were commonplace throughout Afghanistan.

But the security threat in rural areas kept most development organizations from traveling into the hinterlands where the projects were implemented. Instead of local on-site coordination and oversight, USAID and other development organizations used outside partners to do the implementation. These organizations were often huge contracting outfits that did large-scale development all over the world. Many times they hired labor that was not local. Often they would exclude local clans from the very projects meant to benefit them. This contract society approach did not go over well in honor-based, status society.

"In early 2007, U.S. and British defense officials were reported to have estimated that up to half of all aid to Afghanistan failed to reach the right people," says Giustozzi.[8]

To overcome the perceived lack of economic development responsiveness in Afghan rural areas, the military got into the development game. Creating a program known as Commanders Emergency Relief Program (CERP), the U.S. used economic development as a weapon system. That oxymoron should have been an indicator we were on the wrong path. Instead, coalition forces spent exorbitant amounts of money at local levels to dig wells, build schools and clinics, and pave roads. Some units used these projects to gain intelligence on Taliban whereabouts.

While admittedly faster than many USAID actions, many of these projects did long-term harm to Afghan society. For example, "cash for work" created a culture of dependence among once fiercely independent rural people. As part of Pashtun tribal society, there was an economic development tradition known as *Hashar*. Under this code, village elders mobilized the community to clean waterways, clear fields, and even build structures.[9] That concept is gone today.

As the culture of dependence grew, the traditional systems for economic development faded. "In one fell swoop, 'cash for work' programs destroyed our tribal system by paying rural farmers large amounts of money to clean a waterway they would have cleaned anyway," said Deputy Rural Development Minister Tariq Ismati.[10] Even the most rural areas came to expect high sums of money for doing work they once did as part of their community obligations.

Top-down economic development like this widened the trust gap between contract and status society and increased existing tensions between clan society, the coalition, and the Afghan government. It also created new sources of instability, which were locally exploited by violent extremists.

I'm from the government, how ya like me so far?

Has anyone ever tried to sell you something that disgusted you? That's what happened as we crafted a master narrative advocating the Afghan government as the solution to Afghanistan's problems. We tried to push a formal government that was distrusted and hated by most rural Afghans.

"We confused good governance with government. We underestimated the capability and will of local communities to govern themselves," said Ted Callahan.[11] According to Barfield, "Governance is defined as the manner in which communities regulate themselves to preserve social order and maintain their security. Government is the action of the ruling with a continuous exercise of state authority over the population it governs."[12]

The differences between these two definitions lie at the heart of understanding the differences between status and contract society.

Our civilian advisors worked at all formal levels with Afghan ministry technocrats, provincial governors, and district governors. But there was little focus on capacity building within the severely degraded governance structures at the community level.

To make things worse, we re-empowered the warlords who had torn Afghanistan's societal fabric apart during the civil war. We placed them in positions of political power at all levels. This deepened the distrust between rural Afghans and their government, eroded local confidence in us, and opened the door for extremists to take over.

"Imagine a district police chief was assigned by Kabul and the police under him were robbers," said one Wardak villager. "They plundered, looted and raided houses. People became angry and to take revenge, they stood against him and his group. The Taliban used this opportunity...our district is all Taliban now. The people support them."[13]

The coalition campaign not only lost momentum early on, but also marginalized large swaths of clan society, where almost 80 percent of the population resided.

"Criticism vented at the foreign contingents involved in the counterinsurgency has focused on a reliance on massive firepower, mostly derived from the air, a lack of attention for developing local knowledge and familiarity, and failure to maintain whatever knowledge was accumulated through the successive rotations of personnel," writes Giustozzi.[14]

By promoting enemy attrition, large-scale economic development, and a corrupt government, we detached ourselves from local realities and made relative stability unattainable. Our organizational structure was so complicated, however, that we were institutionally blind to the negative impact these top-down effects were having, before it was too late.

Organizational complexity

Our coalition structure, process, and norms in Afghanistan often inhibited effective action. Have you ever seen a NATO coalition organizational chart of Afghanistan? The hierarchical line and block charts, which are supposed to easily communicate chain of command and command authority, instead make your head spin. Try asking for a stability resource, such as a hydrologist, while working in a remote village. It's almost impossible to find one, even though many are on hand.

In the first decade of the Afghan campaign, the same trust gap that existed between the Afghan government and its people emerged in our own coalition with devastating inefficiencies. The bloated structure is one of the key reasons we were unable to discover our own shortcomings and create a locally accepted approach to stabilizing Afghanistan.

More clan feuds festered within our massive, modern government organizations than in rural Pashtun tribal areas of Afghanistan. There were tensions between conventional military forces and SOF. Department of State ran afoul of military COIN objectives. USAID was often at odds with Department of State proponents at the Country Team level. American counterterror and coalition stability operations were in conflict with each other across the country. Coalition forces were distrusted and resented by their Afghan Security Force counterparts. These were but a few of the numerous tensions originating from inside our lumbering, coalition counterinsurgency structure and process.

Numerous vertical layers and horizontal seams separated organizations. These layers were perfectly fine if you were fighting a set-piece battle within traditional maneuver warfare. But this wasn't a traditional campaign. It was a rural insurgency that required strategic resources at local levels.

Our hierarchical layers within our own commands created virtual canyons between the warrior who was the problem owner in the village and the staff officer who held the potential resource solution. Many stability problems in rural Afghanistan required solutions beyond the scope of tactical commanders. But the resources, authorities, and knowledge to address these localized problems usually resided at very senior levels. So if a tactical commander encountered a complex problem, he'd have to go through five or six levels of his chain of command just to get some type of external solution.

The zero-defect mentality ran strong in military command channels. Rather than report the hard-truth, ground-level facts, commanders at the levels above the problem owner often filtered reports with "modified" information meant to make the next level of command happy. Telling the emperor (or in this case, a senior leader) that he's butt naked in the sands of Afghanistan was not a viable course of action among most subordinate military and civilian leaders. Rendering bad news or contrarian viewpoints to the chain of command, even if it was intended to provide leaders with perspective on local reality, was a quick path to a short career in government service.

Organizational seams were equally challenging. The natural communication gaps that often exist between organizations were more pronounced. These group tensions were more common in organizations that had different charters but "played in the same sandbox." For instance, there were rivalries between conventional and Special Operations Forces working in the same geographic battle space. There were also turf wars between USAID, which had economic development capacity but little access to rural areas, and Special Forces units, who had local access to communities but very limited economic development expertise.

Just as Afghan tribes would compete over perceived scarcity of water and land, these groups would compete for scarce authorities, budget, and even perceived status. If relationships were poor, the seams were wider. If relationships were sound, the seams weren't as big and collaboration was possible. Clash of clans, anyone?

One of the major problems with all of these varied actors, gaps, and seams was that it was almost impossible to achieve unity of effort, or even unity of understanding on the wicked problems facing the coalition. The stability arena was such a cluttered maze, it was difficult to even identify who the players were and what they could offer to solve a problem. The result of all this organizational complexity was a massive structure that couldn't get out of its own way in finding a long-term solution to Afghan instability.

A stability crossroads

This is where we found ourselves at the end of 2008. Every time I drove past that Soviet equipment boneyard, it haunted me more and more. The

Taliban had grown immensely powerful. Haqqani attacks were increasing in Kabul and in the east. Evidence mounted of al Qa'ida re-emerging in the country as well. After almost a decade of counterinsurgency in Afghanistan, we needed a new approach.

U.S. Army Special Forces began to take note of these shortcomings and put forward a new plan. What happened next was the evolution of a stability framework that offered novel ways to defeat violent extremists in Afghanistan and beyond. In the next section we will see how this untenable disadvantage with violent extremists caused us to change the game and go local in Afghanistan.

Chapter Highlights

- *The first decade of the Afghan campaign was an ineffective top-down counterinsurgency approach that enabled powerful extremist control by 2009.*

- *Security was focused on man hunting, not building host nation capacity.*

- *Economic development was too big and locally out of touch, and it marginalized minority clans.*

- *Governance was only focused on contract society formal structures that were perceived as illegitimate by local clans; an emphasis on informal status society governance was not included, but was expected by the majority of Afghans.*

- *Our coalition had no central narrative that resonated with Afghans or our people at home.*

- *Our coalition organizational structure was so complex that it hindered our actions and processes, widened the trust gap between contract and status society, and empowered extremist relevance with critical local populations.*

- *Many of our interorganizational problems stemmed from internal feuds and clan-like rivalries. It turns out that even in contract society, we exhibit more clan tendencies than we realize — we just aren't aware of it.*

PART II

CHANGING THE GAME

Chapter 5

Finding Lawrence

"Do not try too much with your own hands. Better the Arabs do it tolerably than that you do it perfectly."

— T.E. Lawrence, 27 Articles

Kandahar Province, January 2010

"Sir, I think we may have to abort this mission."

Green Beret Captain Robby was about to brief Brigadier General Reeder that they were looking at possible mission failure in their task: embedding into one of the most difficult districts in Kandahar Province. "These guys don't want us in their village. They won't even make eye contact when we patrol through the market."

It was a daunting challenge. They were trying to establish bottom-up stability in an area hard-hit by years of conflict. Tribal tensions were running high and the district government ignored them. Robby's men were outgunned and outnumbered. Their compound on the edge of the village was regularly attacked by Taliban fighters and their intelligence said they were under threat of even more catastrophic attacks.

Reeder's concern was evident. "Okay, I get it. If you want to close it down, I understand. What do you want to do?"

Robby took another breath and said, "Sir, give us 90 days. If we can't do it by then, we'll shut it down."

Within 60 days these Green Berets turned the whole thing around.

The program was so successful that it was one of the deciding factors in ISAF Commander General Stan McChrystal throwing his full weight behind going local as a strategic program.

So how did this Special Forces team go from 'zero' to 'hero' in such a short time?

First, Captain Robby created space for his men to operate inside the village. Despite being surrounded on all sides, Robby's men fought the Taliban surgically and aggressively. They patrolled the village and surrounding farms tirelessly to push out their operating "white space."

But while conducting these patrols, Captain Robby pushed his men to do more than just look for bad guys. They worked to identify what was destabilizing the area. Each team member, during every patrol, was responsible for asking locals questions and fact-finding along the way. Often locals would share things with lower-ranking team members that they would not share with the team commander.

After patrols, Robby would hold team "fireside chats": collaborative discussions to share the knowledge and insights on relationships and interpersonal dynamics gained during the patrol. No detail was too small. No team member was left out.

Slowly, the real sources of instability in the village came into focus.

One was simmering tension between the majority tribe that owned all the land and the minority landless tribe that was subsistence farming on the village outskirts. Rather than host the shouting matches that had been the norm up until this point, Robby now met with the tribes separately and built trust as mediators.

Poor water management was causing severe agricultural problems for both factions. Neither tribe, however, could get past their honor-based feuds to repair the shared waterway and increase agricultural yields. With advice and technical assistance from coalition civilians, and District Center and USAID experts on agriculture and hydrology, Captain Robby used his newfound credibility to persuade each rival tribal leader to work on his respective part of the waterway until the waterway connected.

Before long, both tribal leaders were participating in district governor meetings, speaking with one voice on their issues and needs with the Afghan government, and local defense forces were recruiting from the village.

By the time his men departed Afghanistan in June 2014, Captain Robby's VSO site was the subject of multiple training videos, several *Washington Post* profile pieces, and multiple interagency best practice reports. More importantly, the resilient tribal leaders from both tribes were re-engaged in local leadership while Taliban fighters steered far clear of this village.

What did this mission require? Advisors with numerous and diverse skills. Technical skills. Personal traits like patience, perseverance, and maturity.

In this case, these men were the right men for the job. So how do we find — or build —more of these right people?

More than methodology...

Counterinsurgency expert Andrew Exum writes "going local is predicated upon implementation by a bunch of geniuses."[1]

I don't agree with his assessment. We don't need geniuses, but we do need to put the right people against the problem.

Who it takes

While there are many players in destabilized areas, the most critical person is the advisor. I use the term here to apply to any private or public sector practitioner working at the local level to foster stability: corporate representatives, law enforcement, government civilians, or military personnel. What distinguishes an advisor is this — in the rough areas, they are the folks closest to the local problems, connecting bottom to top.

Today's advisor cannot afford to be one-dimensional; the environment is far too complicated and dangerous for that. Today's advisors must be a hybrid of core competencies.

Who is the person best suited for these complex challenges? Well, to put it in simple terms, the perfect person will be a combination of Jason Bourne, T.E. Lawrence, and the Verizon Guy!

Competency Trait 1: Using Jason Bourne's surgical lethality to create "white space"

In the Bourne series of books and movies, Jason Bourne is a CIA operative who has been betrayed by his handlers and labeled as rogue. He must make his way across international borders and through hostile cities to find his enemies and clear his name. Despite run-ins with law enforcement, assassins, and unwitting civilians, Bourne always applies just the right amount of violence to resolve each conflict he faces without making the situation worse than it already is.

Going local is not some feel-good, "We Are the World" program: Lethality, applied proportionally, is a necessity to create the needed space for local stability. Violence and forced coercion are primary tools in the advisor's kit and an unfortunate requirement in these dangerous spaces.

If oppressed communities stand on their own again, violent extremists would become irrelevant; therefore the intimidation they apply is relentless. They will never sit idly by and let this happen.

Nongovernmental groups and charities would do it if they could, but even the most well-resourced projects become targets. Joanne Herring, the famed Houston oil heiress from the movie *Charlie Wilson's War*, learned just how bad intimidation can be. Her charity recently sponsored a Pashtun village in western Afghanistan. Things were going great until the project became too successful and threatened the local extremists. The project manager was promptly murdered, citizens threatened, and the project delayed indefinitely. I have seen dozens of these types of examples, and they are getting worse.

While lethality is needed, we often overuse it. If we've learned anything in this long war, it's that we can't kill our way to victory. Even if we took the gloves off and pursued total war, the likelihood of body-count warfare defeating this type of shadowy foe is very slim. Until that day, lethality should be surgical and precise.

Advisors cannot afford to be singularly focused on lethality. "We need to create a culture where raids are not synonymous with special operations," says Linda Robinson of Special Operations Forces working in outlying communities."[2] Direct action missions, raids, and man hunting are only responsible if they are in support of larger bottom-up stability missions. Otherwise, they just push extremists deeper into the populace and the populace further from us.

Police Chief Kelly McMillin, a 'go local' law enforcement officer in Salinas, California, told me that the only time his embedded officers in the Hebbron neighborhood lost rapport with locals was when they made arrests or raided houses.[3] It violated their hard-earned trust with the locals whom they worked with day after day. Numerous Green Berets in Afghanistan had similar aversions to raiding homes in villages where they lived and worked. Instead they leveraged outside special operators to conduct the raids or even local village leaders to talk the wanted suspects out.

This is hard for many in the security community to deal with, but is indicative of the type of maturity and tactical self-restraint needed to do this type of work.

For those advisors itching for a fight, we will find ourselves in plenty of scrapes with violent extremists. But lethality must be the means to an end, not the end in of itself.

Competency Trait 2: Find your 'inner Lawrence' to work among the locals

Going local enables us to build a level of legitimacy that can achieve strategic results not possible when we only project into extremist safe havens from the top down.

T.E. Lawrence, or "Lawrence of Arabia," understood this well. He was an advisor to the Bedouin tribes in the Middle East during World War I. A controversial figure accused of "going native" by some, he nevertheless was a Game Changer. Although an excellent fighter, he excelled at working with indigenous populations. Lawrence promoted stability from the grass-roots level, one tribe at a time, and overcame not only complex tribal environments but even more complicated challenges within his own Western coalition. He advanced a master narrative of freedom from the Ottoman Turks, which mobilized tens of thousands of Arab tribesmen — normally at each other's throats — to action, while simultaneously convincing the British government to support his unorthodox efforts.

Unconventional Lawrencian traits he used to do this include:

- Deep study of local history and tribal culture

- Negotiations

- Storytelling

- Group dynamics

- Active listening.

To change the game we have to find our "inner Lawrence." These skills are not intuitive to many advisors. Lethality training gets plenty of resource attention, but these indirect skills receive little training focus at all, despite their importance and the fact that they require intense training and preparation.[4]

Competency Trait 3: The Verizon Guy connects 'top' to 'bottom'

Most of us have seen the Verizon commercials with the Verizon Guy. (Although now the little traitor has moved to Sprint.) An unassuming guy in a Verizon uniform, with a cell phone to his ear, has a group of people following him around as he goes from place to place asking, "Can you hear me now?"[5]

Simple and amusing. But at a closer look, the Verizon Guy may be exactly the type of person we need to promote collaboration in complex organizational structures and to close trust gaps inside and outside our organizations.

1. He's connected. The Verizon Guy has a massive network backing him up. He can bridge organizational seams. He is connected to all relevant participants in a complex problem. If he's not, he'll pop up in a new place where he can connect.

The Verizon Guy loves connecting people. He is always bringing people together. It's as much a part of his personality as Bourne's lethality and Lawrence's tradecraft. He trains intensively in collaboration, and the process is part of his DNA.

2. He likes rough spots. The Verizon Guy embraces ambiguity. He goes to the roughest places on earth to ensure that those around him are connected. By doing so, he identifies gaps, challenges, and opportunities. Senior leaders value his access. He is a critical and strategic asset for overcoming trust gaps.

3. He reaches back in real time. The Verizon Guy's network — his tribe — walks behind him into every rough spot he enters. They are always there to reach back to for support, technical expertise, or perhaps another connection to someone who can help.

4. His people above him are accountable down to him. No matter where his tribe goes, they are happily accountable down to him. It's all about the network. No matter how deep he goes into the rough areas, he never forgets his strategic role as a catalyst and connector.

It's not easy becoming the Verizon Guy. (In this book we will call him a catalyst.) It requires an understanding of complex environments, self-awareness, collaboration skills, and a range of other skill sets. Many don't understand it and unfortunately many others, including senior leaders, are threatened by it.

Special Operations Forces, in particular, will need to grow into this role around the world. "The biggest future impact of Special Forces may not be in combat but in partnering and networking," wrote David Ignatius in an article describing the future role of SOF."[6]

Advising — not an equal-opportunity profession

Advising is not for everyone. It takes a certain kind of individual. In the Special Operations community, the Green Berets have a unique capacity for this kind of work. Department of State Bureau of Conflict and Stabilization Operations (CSO) and USAID Office of Transition Initiative (OTI) are also two organizations with the right charter and mindset. Corporations and law enforcement have similar folks who are especially suited for local work in rough areas.

I'm not saying that conventional forces, Department of State, or USAID shouldn't do this work. Nor am I saying that conventional forces doing combat advisor missions aren't viable missions. But any organization that works in these rough areas, regardless of title or background, must be accountable for training to the standard of what's required.

Many organizations do not train their people like Special Forces does, yet they insist on inserting them into these unforgiving clan societies. To advise in these complex environments, conventional military and law enforcement must carefully screen their advisors. Salinas Police Chief Kelly McMillin told me he selects his embedded law enforcement officers based on maturity and how they value relationship building.

Any private or public organization intending to go local should embrace our hybrid Jason Bourne–T.E. Lawrence–Verizon Guy model and train intensely for it.

Beware of 'that guy'

Here is who we *don't* need for this type of work: those who wear patches like "Major League Infidel" and utter phrases like "booger eaters." People who don't have the strategic maturity and environmental patience to work at local levels should not be put into these situations.

This is a growing problem. We still need folks to do badass fighting, but they have to have the maturity to switch on and off as their operational environment changes.

Even some personnel within Special Forces and Special Operations Forces lack the skills for this type of advisory work, or selfishly choose not to do it in favor of stroking their own ego through lethal targeting. Similar challenges of pursuing unconventional tradecraft exist in traditional diplomacy and development circles.

Finding the right person who meets local advising requirements is a leadership issue and requires moral courage from all leaders involved.

"This mission will fail," says Special Forces Captain Trey, "if an outlier exists on the team. He risks creating issues for the team's success."[7]

What it takes: understanding the "human domain"

"The neglect or misjudgment of population-centric considerations in U.S. strategic calculations is easily documented," say senior leaders in the Marine Corps, Army, and U.S. Special Operations in a recent Pentagon document.[8] "Time and again, the U.S. has undertaken to engage in conflict without fully considering the physical, cultural, and social environments that comprise what some have called the 'human domain.'"

Having the right person is not enough — there are specific skills and knowledge that require mastery for even the most naturally talented advisors. If having the right person provides the 'art,' we also need to provide the 'science' to develop the game-changing tradecraft.

The strategic selector switch

All of these innate qualities — Bourne lethality, Lawrencian tradecraft, and Verizon Guy connectivity — are important components of the modern advisor going local. But knowing when and how to apply them, and in what combination, is what really makes advisors strategic. This is the internal selector switch, the discernment that lets us toggle from one trait to the other.

Today's advisor must be able to transition between these distinct roles as effortlessly as a chameleon moves along and changes colors in a dense jungle full of circling, hungry birds.

There will be times when advisors or leaders must kill, arrest, or capture irreconcilable types. At other times, stability will require deep appreciation for local culture, history, and what is destabilizing the area. Still other times require connections to be made across groups as diverse as farming villages and embassy diplomats.

Mastery of this internal selector switch requires deep preparation and training.

Deep preparation

Deep preparation involves developing training scenarios where these three advisor capabilities are employed in the most challenging conditions. We must go deeper, broader than cursory classes on culture or survival language classes. This is new in most training environments that have been focused for far too long on arrests and shooting our way out of problems.

The now-extinct USSOCOM–sponsored Academic Week was a good model for deep preparation. "Academic Week was very unique," said Major Gene, a Civil Affairs major. "We left that week understanding how much we didn't know and what we needed to work on for our pre-deployment training."[9]

During that training, Afghan government officials, USAID representatives, and even people from nonprofit organizations came to train our Marines, SEALs, and Green Berets. Some operators winced at this, but most saw the utility. The really good advisors know when to shut up and listen to people who know what they're talking about, no matter where they come from.

To leverage their "inner Lawrence," advisors must broaden their skill set to include the time-tested tasks of negotiations, tribal dynamics, storytelling, agriculture, and dispute resolution.

All deep preparation is underscored with the Lawrencian attitude of humility and self-awareness. We have much to learn, no matter how many times we've been 'over there.' The opposite of this is what Special Operations call tactical arrogance. You know the attitude: "I have already been there so I have it figured out."

Make no mistake — this is an enemy! Arrogance can be deadly. Arrogance can cause mission failure.

A word to leaders...

To change the game and go local, we need more involvement from senior leaders in the private and public sector. This includes our politicians. But because most of today's foreign stability problems are local, senior leaders are far removed from them.

Don't let this stand.

As a senior leader, you have resources and authority to prevent distance and bureaucracy from keeping you away from local relevance. But you must insist on accountability down to the lowest level at all times.

The only thing worse than tactical arrogance is strategic or policy arrogance from generals, diplomats, and politicians. There are senior leaders who are literally insulted when approached as a student on this type of training. However, *there is no rank, status, or demanding calendar that renders you above the need to deeply prepare.*

The first step is for leaders to embrace the merits of going local. It then requires an understanding of how our society differs from theirs in the ways previously spelled out, and this requires them to be students. Do this as a leader, and you'll earn immediate respect. If you fail to do this — or if you outsource your preparation to subordinates — you risk our failure.

The village stability program went mainstream in Afghanistan because Brigadier General Miller developed a master narrative and sold it to key senior leaders, politicians, and members of the media. *He empowered everyone in his tribe to tell the story.*

Senior leaders must also provide "top cover" to bottom-up efforts when partner governments don't want U.S. involvement in outlying areas or can't get past their own agendas. This is where skills in statecraft, corporate senior-level influence, and military-to-military relationships are vital.

Senior leaders can go local in your own way: government and corporate bureaucracies are often like clans or tribes — warring internally, protecting turf, fighting for resources. Convince them. Empathize with them. Persuade them. Remind them that, regardless of organizational affiliation, we all need the same thing: collaboration on these hard problems.

Going local also requires our leaders to build master narratives with their foreign partners. In Iraq for example, persuade the Shia-dominated government to profess long-term commitment and empowerment of marginalized Sunni communities. They should proclaim these narratives to ISIS boldly and fearlessly.

We need leaders to:

- Value the Game Changer tradecraft;

- Be accountable to the embedded advisors and honor-based communities they help;

- Run top-cover for our advisors and teach their foreign partners to do the same.

We must redefine our environment

We need to change how we frame the problem at a big-picture level. In order to respond to the needs of a rapidly changing world, "a shift toward a more strategic security framework using a fragile state lens would represent a vast improvement from the over-militarized, short time frame, counterinsurgency and counterterror lens we use now," says Pauline Baker. "It would enable U.S. policy to have more flexibility, credibility, and opportunity for sustainable outcomes."[10]

For the U.S. government, the concept has been historically known as Foreign Internal Defense (FID). FID is the whole-of-nation approach for defeating extremism, insurgency, and lawlessness by working with partner nations. FID is an excellent national vehicle for security and stability abroad that we have, unfortunately, all but forgotten since the 9/11 attacks.

Extremist threats in honor-based clan areas, however, require a modified FID model that includes local advising work in clan society and advising irregular forces. Leaders should accept that counterterror operations and counterinsurgency operations work under the context of the longer-term FID mission. Law enforcement and private corporations should have similar broad campaigns that exercise all their capabilities working together in status and contract society.

By, with, through

Our advisors can't do it all. Nor should they have to. There will be times when our presence at a local level is not possible or advisable. Most countries have indigenous special operations forces or special police that are well suited for this type of local advisory duty. In a pinch, such as with the Afghan National Army Special Forces, they can be created for this purpose. But a responsible, vetted partner nation unit to work among locals is a necessity for the Game Changer approach to work.

This means we will have to carefully select and groom the indigenous partners with whom we work. We will have to change how we train host nation forces for this kind of work. The traditional infantry-training regimen we give our partners doesn't go far enough.

Even if you don't use these principles for yourself, consider how they can serve you as training content when working with partner forces. If we work with partner forces to help them embed into outlying communities, behave responsibly, stay in tune with the local population, and use these Game Changer tactics, we will not have to do all the work ourselves.

We are falling behind violent extremists because we are not always sending the right people, and we're not giving the right people our best stuff for preparation. We have to lean on those most capable of overcoming our own government and corporate inefficiencies so that we can help communities push out extremists and criminals on their own.

Chapter Highlights

- *These immensely complex and dangerous environments require a special person with unique skills.*

- *The advisor best suited for today's complex challenges will be a combination of Jason Bourne, T.E. Lawrence, and the Verizon Guy.*

- *Jason Bourne–style surgical lethality gives us the ability to push back against intimidation and create operational space.*

- *T.E. Lawrence–style going local is at the heart of our bottom-up tradecraft.*

- *The Verizon Guy spans the globe increasing the communication reach of a diverse network rallying around solving complex stability problems.*

- *Today's advisor must have an internal selector switch that enables him to toggle between these distinct skill sets.*

- *Advisor tradecraft must be multidisciplinary, authentic, and part of our DNA.*

- *Leaders can't allow the tyranny of distance and top-down bureaucracy to keep us from local relevance. This means senior leader accountability down to the lowest level at all times through trust and empowerment.*

- *Deep preparation should include situations that test advisor ability to apply the right skills in the right conditions.*

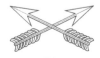

Chapter 6

The Game Changer Framework

Return to Nagahan Village

As our UH-60 Black Hawk helicopter banked for its final approach into the landing zone at Nagahan Village, you could sense the energy on the ground, even from 1,500 feet up.

A lot had changed in the year since my visit to this original VSO site in the fertile Arghandab River Valley. The special operations experimental program known as Community Defense Initiative (CDI) had ballooned into the strategic program known as Village Stability Operations (VSO), and Afghan Local Police (ALP). What had started with a handful of Green Beret advisors and ragtag Afghan volunteers had escalated into a Ministry of Interior program, which was climbing in strength to more than 10,000 local police and providing vast coverage of Afghan rural areas.

Today, this nondescript village would be the first village in southern Afghanistan to formally enroll its local defenders as ALP under the Ministry of Interior. The Afghan government and the NATO coalition would validate this local defense force, issue uniforms, pay them, and begin a new security focus in southern Afghanistan.

This was a big day. Tribal elders, government officials, coalition leaders, and hundreds of curious villagers were converging on the small mud compound that had housed this Green Beret VSO site since its inception.

As the aircraft tossed and lurched in the crisp November air, I reflected on all the things Nagahan Village had endured since we started going local here.

In 2008, after the death of the resilient tribal leader, Mullah Naqibullah, who'd held stability in place for decades, the village and its district were unraveling from the bottom up. Extremists were obtaining unprecedented influence by leveraging intra-tribal feuds and other sources of instability on the outskirts of Kandahar City. Still, pockets of resistance remained, and some leaders quietly asked for coalition assistance.

A small Special Forces team led by Captain Trey convinced several Alikozai elders to allow the team to get surrounded — on purpose — and move into the village of Nagahan. Once they were embedded, the Green Berets met locals and helped them establish a local defense force.

In the spring of 2010, just a few months later, the replacement team of Green Berets, led by Captain Joe, endured several setbacks, including the loss of their dynamic team sergeant, Master Sergeant Mark Coleman, to an improvised explosive device. Nagahan also experienced a devastating suicide bomb attack at a local wedding that killed and maimed numerous civilians. Undaunted, the Nagahan villagers and the Special Forces team continued to stand up on their own.

By summer's end, the next Special Forces team in Nagahan, led by Captain Rob, took the local program to the next level. Local security grew. Extremists avoided the village when traveling through the area. Green Berets spent more time patrolling through Nagahan and learning about local grievances. The Green Berets collaborated with outside organizations to address these grievances, which led to increased local resiliency and self-sufficiency.

Local advisors implemented participatory community development, including agricultural and hydrology initiatives. Informal governance re-emerged in place of Taliban shadow courts. Tribal elders who had been largely silent in the first year saw activities shift from a security-focused initiative to a broader, stability-focused effort.

Going local in Nagahan Village led to stability from the bottom up. It expanded to other villages along the Arghandab River. Extremist activity receded considerably throughout Arghandab District, and commerce improved. Freedom of movement between the farmers of Nagahan and Kandahar City was once again unhindered, to pre-2008 levels. Contract and status society were starting to close the trust gap and connect in ways that were more natural and locally appropriate.

Once the village stability platform was fully established, the SOF team notified the NATO coalition that the community leaders were ready to validate their local defenders to the Ministry of Interior and take on the official mantle of Afghan Local Police, or ALP. Six months before, this type of connection to contract society would have caused a bottom-up village revolt and a top-down cold shoulder from the Kabul government.

When going local, timing is everything. These SOF advisors waited until village resiliency was in place, extremists marginalized, and local relationships between advisors and the community solidified. Only then did they leverage their own credibility with local leaders to persuade them to connect to the government through the ALP program.

Expanding this program and achieving strategic outcomes isn't as daunting as we might think. What happened in Nagahan Village wasn't magic. It was a disciplined application of a game-changing framework, which can be, and was scaled up and replicated throughout Afghanistan in remarkably short order. Nagahan Village was just one of many villages across Afghanistan to go through this stability transformation, which cumulatively improved Afghan stability and degraded extremist effectiveness from 2010 to 2012.

Let's look a little deeper at the macro-level effects, good and bad, that going local achieved in Afghanistan, starting with the shortfalls.

Effects of VSO and ALP

Like any initiative applied in complex environments, the VSO–ALP program was far from perfect. Both programs had problems, and in some cases were downright counterproductive. Going local had many skeptics, including Afghan President Karzai, Human Rights Watch, OXFAM, other nonprofit organizations, and individual opponents within the Afghan and coalition governments.

These skeptics and challengers advanced some extremely important criticisms to address and learn from, many of which have already been integrated into an enhanced approach of going local. Some of the more significant challenges are:

1. Going local fosters instability.

2. Going local undermines the legitimacy of the state.

3. Going local is not sustainable.

4. Going local cannot be expanded.

These are all valid arguments, advanced by a range of diligent and concerned stakeholders. Let's look closer at each one.

Challenge 1: Going local fosters instability.

Militias tend to upset people. Rogue militias and illegally armed groups are pervasive concerns among human rights groups, nonprofits, politicians, government civilians, and the military.

A major concern is that local groups like Afghan Local Police, created "to achieve short-term goals…are again being armed without adequate oversight or accountability." This quote comes from the group Human Rights Watch in a piece entitled *Just Don't Call It a Militia*. It is one of the most extensive works out there opposing local defense programs.[1]

Human Rights Watch reported several alleged abuses and issues with militias and Afghan Local Police from five different provinces. However, the number was minimal compared to the number of local sites operating around the country. The other significant factor the report did not consider was that the number of abuses conducted by regular Afghan police are equally, if not more egregious.

There's no denying that local behavior among most Afghan security forces is a real challenge. Whether it's Afghan National Army, Afghan National Police, or Afghan Local Police, you don't have to look hard to find abuse of locals. The danger of abusive and predatory behavior by militia units is a real and valid issue that must be addressed.

Going local in Afghanistan, at least in the 2010 SOF approach, was never intended to become an accelerated program for creating large militia numbers to cover a coalition military exit. The original premise of VSO, indeed the overarching principle for going local in general, is to work long-term within status society to create space for resilient clan leaders to stand on their own across all lines of stability, not just security. Going local requires responsible oversight, a clear demobilization and assimilation plan for security forces, and above all, a locally appropriate connection to the formal government. Which brings us to the second challenge, that going local threatens formal institutions.

Challenge 2: Going local undermines the legitimacy of the state.

Human Rights Watch, OXFAM, Kabul politicians, and a range of others claim that going local undermines political legitimacy of the formal government. This is a valid concern, especially when considering the particularly turbulent period of the Afghan civil war in the 1990s. Brutal warlords and armed groups literally tore the fabric of Afghan society to shreds. There are several points to addressing this challenge, starting with local reality.

Emphasis on a formal government that promotes individual liberty and rule of law is noble but extremely out of touch with local reality in places where violent extremists thrive. It is often the very absence of state capacity that enables violent extremists to exploit degraded clan society and project violence against that government and others around the globe.

Most of these status societies will likely remain unmanageable by the state for a very long period. Honor and feud within these clan-based societies will continue to dominate the stability landscape where the government can't reach. Acknowledging and working locally within the legitimate form of governance and security, even if it is tribal or rule of the clan, is a reality we must face if we are going to deny safe haven to violent extremists bent on doing us more harm than ever.

With this reality in mind, we should deeply consider the cautions made by these organizations about the legitimacy of state rule. While it's critical to work within these clan realities, we need to be careful that we continue to seek locally appropriate connections with the government of that area.

There are some special operators and stability practitioners who believe that the honor-based societies and clan behavior of tribal areas should be the sole focus of the bottom-up effort. This would be the "One Tribe at a Time" approach advanced by Major Jim Gant. In other words, once we move into local communities and help them stand up against intimidation, this is the end of our effort. Leave them be.

I disagree, and so do a range of others who see the "rule of the clan" as ultimately disruptive to long-term stability in civil society. The local approach is more than tribes. It includes the broader categories of clans and communities governed by status society. It helps exploited areas get past the primary identities of gangs or tribes, which promote honor-based conflict. Instead, it encourages, over time and through local relationships, developing secondary identities that foster a broader community network of local resiliency, and eventually contract society, to solve problems.

Promoting tribalism or clan society as the only form of governance is not in the best interest of the host nation or our national security. Yes, we need to inject local reality into our actions. And that will often include working with and supporting tribes and clans for very long periods of time.

This is not a matter of government vs. clan — it's a matter of timing. It's embracing what local reality already demands. For the immediate future, no matter how much various human rights groups call for governments to assert the rule of law into clan society, the local population will resist these connections between status and contract society at every turn.

We must first help exploited communities stand on their own, win their trust, and then walk them back to the state. This re-establishment of trust between community and government ultimately renders violent extremists irrelevant.

In many places this may take decades, or longer. We need to adjust our expectations of time, not our endgame of balanced relative stability. We should work with clan society on a much longer timeline than we currently allow under typical interventions in Iraq and Afghanistan. Going forward, we should always acknowledge and embrace the difficulty, complexity, and ultimately the goodness that comes from connecting status and contract society.

Challenge 3: Going local is not sustainable.

"This seems like a really impressive program but it doesn't seem sustainable over the long term," a Congressional staffer told me when visiting Afghanistan in the summer of 2010. This common concern is usually put forth by politicians, senior military officers, and others distantly removed from the local realities of Afghanistan and other at-risk areas.

Going local focuses on meeting people where they are, not where we want them to be. In terms of local buy-in and popular support, this approach is a much more sustainable option than projecting a large military footprint and contract society biases for short durations, only to return en masse when the undergoverned area collapses on itself, as happened in 2014 with ISIS in Iraq.

A second component to this argument goes like this: "The real test of the impact for the ALP in terms of insurgent presence and attacks will take place when the presence of international forces is reduced."[2] This passage by Human Rights Watch summarizes a major shortfall of Afghan Local Police that must be corrected for going local in the future. As with the above concerns, this can only be addressed by long-term presence and oversight.

The final element of this challenge was mentioned in Chapter 5, regarding what I call the 'genius paradox' advanced by COIN expert Andrew Exum. The concern is that going local can only be done by a very limited number of people who happen to have uncommon skills. While this local approach isn't for everyone, there are plenty of people in the private and public sectors more than capable of going local better than our violent extremist enemies. In addition, by the end of Part II of this book, it will be quite obvious that the mindset and skills needed to succeed in this endeavor can be identified, institutionalized, cultivated, and trained.

Challenge 4: Going local cannot be expanded.

This challenge usually comes from tacit supporters who like the approach, but don't believe there are enough advisors to achieve strategic reach. The growth of VSO from a tactical science project, which barely garnered the attention of coalition generals, into what ISAF Commander General David Petraeus called "arguably the most critical element in our effort to help Afghanistan develop the capability to secure itself," illustrates the propensity for growth.[3]

The caution, as it is advanced by a range of skeptics, is in how it grows. Clearly, Afghan Local Police took on a growth rate that far exceeded the pace of the local populace, and violated many of the basic tenets of going local. At the heart of this is a problem that must be understood by senior leaders and strategists. It is this:

Strategic solutions within extremist-dominated safe havens require persistence and local presence. Going local for short-term gain or expanding local defense forces without close vetting and support of local resilient leaders is a recipe for disaster.

Finally, regarding this challenge, there is a recurring theme that continues to be overlooked. The expansion potential for going local is indeed limited when it is confined to unilateral U.S. and Western actions. However, the ability to go local grows exponentially with the integration of vetted partner nation security forces to assist in the effort.

In fact, building capacity for well-behaved partner nation security forces, police, and special operations forces who can work in clan society with irregular groups, not only increases trust, but also government reach and legitimacy in locally appropriate ways.

To grow this partner nation capacity, however, requires significant change in U.S. leader mindset and peacetime authorities to train and advise locally in clan society. If we look closer, the argument that going local depends on geniuses and is not scalable is, in reality, a shroud for not wanting to win badly enough to change how we select our people, train our partners, and empower locals to defeat the enemy where he lives.

These four issues make clear that there will be challenges going forward. Despite this, there is compelling evidence from 2010 to 2013 that this approach holds promise for defeating violent extremists well beyond Afghanistan.

Let's examine some of the most significant effects that going local had on violent extremists, Afghan stability, and us.

Going local degraded violent extremist capacity

We knew that going local with VSO was going to be effective for a simple reason: the extremists hated it. It scared the crap out of them. U.S. advisors were living and working among local Afghans. We were on the 'home turf' of the enemy — the Afghan village. Extremists despised the fact that informal governance was filling the void better than Taliban shadow courts, and that local farming capacity and security were also improving.

A recent DOD report stated that VSO and ALP operations had "resulted in security, governance, and development that Taliban Senior Leadership (TBSL), including the Quetta Shura, has identified as a significant threat to their objectives."[4] In a 2013 report on Afghan Local Police, Mark Moyar wrote, "According to enemy sources, insurgent leaders generally viewed the ALP as the foremost obstacle to the success of the insurgency."[5] This program was clearly getting under the skin of violent extremists across Afghanistan.

You could also measure its success by how the enemy did its targeting. Violent extremists concentrated much of their offensive activity against the Afghan Local Police, the security arm of VSO. The suicide wedding bombing in Nagahan Village proved how desperate the extremists were becoming due to VSO.

"VSO and ALP has proven to be a significant threat to the Taliban, which has led them to initiate a campaign of intimidation, assassination, and disruption against ALP members and government officials," claimed Assistant Secretary of Defense for Special Operations and Low Intensity Conflict, Michael A. Sheehan, during his Senate Armed Services testimony.[6]

Violent extremists feared village defenders even more than Afghan army and police forces. Enemy forces targeted three times as many Afghan Local Police as all other Afghan National Security Forces combined.[7]

Yet, going local provided a huge return on investment: ALP training cost a fraction of what it cost to train Afghan National Security Forces. Where many Afghan security forces struggled to hold their ground against extremist attacks, the ALP held their ground 88 percent of the time. Further enhancing the return on investment, the ALP desertion rate was the lowest of any Afghan National Security Force unit, at only 1.1 percent per month.[8]

Going local had significant effects on the Afghan people

"The bottom-up approach was extremely successful and offered a relationship with the Afghans that I haven't seen in other bases with heavy footprints, Hesco barriers, and lots of barbed wire," said Ben Moeling, a senior State Department veteran. Ben would know. He was Director of the Kandahar Provincial Reconstruction Team in 2010 and one of the most influential diplomats in Southern Afghanistan.

Ben was a skeptic at first, until he accompanied a Special Forces team deep into Uruzgan Province as they opened up one of the first VSO sites in what was formerly written off as Taliban territory. After that visit, Ben changed his tune about going local.[9]

For three consecutive years, I conducted thousands of interviews with Afghans about the VSO and ALP programs. I spoke with farmers, shopkeepers, tribal leaders, government officials, and a host of others. I interviewed representatives from almost every tribe where VSO thrived. Most were profoundly in favor of going local and supported any efforts that re-empowered status society.

Afghan villagers were wary of SOF advisors moving into their community in the beginning, unless they were actively resisting violent extremists. However, as these advisors proved their willingness to go to the rooftops and defend not just their own firebase but the village as a whole, the community's perceptions thawed considerably. SOF advisors fought, bled, and in some cases died for these communities.

In an honor-based society this goes a long way.

Going local addressed many of the militia concerns cited earlier in this chapter by re-empowering locally appropriate stability, not just security. "VSO re-energizes what was already there," said senior U.S. leader Tom Baltazar. Tom was the Senior USAID Representative in southern Afghanistan and a tireless advocate for local stability. "History has shown that community policing is the only way you can bring long-term stability to a given region," he concluded.[10]

Afghans were also quite receptive to SOF efforts in helping them re-establish their own local resiliencies. Advisors, for example, coordinated with U.S. Department of Agriculture extension agents to help farmers learn better farming techniques. These seemingly insignificant local actions would pay off the following 'fighting season.'

In the spring of 2011, when Taliban fighters returned from their Pakistan winter refuge to south Afghanistan for the summer fight, there was a clear correlation between villages that pushed these fighters out of their communities with those that had locally improved their food insecurity problem.[11] This not only posed a security risk to the insurgents, but "addressed deeper political, ethnic, tribal, and socioeconomic issues necessary to sustain these gains in the long run," explains Lisa-Saum Manning in a report on Afghan Local Police.[12]

Going local expanded geographic control

The areas where VSO and ALP made these stability and security gains were in the same areas that insurgents relied on for rural safe haven. Five of the six most volatile Afghan provinces had active VSO sites and saw significant drops in coalition fatalities and enemy attacks.[13] Another study stated that the "dramatic and comprehensive shift to VSO that emphasizes the development of security and governance while also eliminating insurgent safe havens is a more likely causal factor."[14]

The expansion capacity of VSO and ALP also became self-evident in short order. Assistant Secretary Sheehan further stated in testimony that "since its inception, VSO has expanded Afghan government influence in key rural areas from 1,000 square kilometers to 23,500 square kilometers today, and has enabled a massive expansion in small-scale infrastructure development in these rural areas."

Going local stabilized critically important but remote areas that were extremist safe havens but beyond the reach of regular security forces. It did this with considerably fewer manpower and equipment resources than those used in conventional COIN activities.

As recently as 2013, an executive summary on ALP stated that with just over 20,810 Afghan Local Police, the force provided security to 17 percent of the Afghan population (5 million people). This document cites a RAND study that credits ALP for reducing insurgent activity by 20 percent within a three-kilometer radius of ALP checkpoints within one year of establishment.[15]

Going local helped defeat the other enemy — ourselves

In addition to degrading violent extremists and promoting relative stability in rural Afghanistan, going local also profoundly affected the second enemy — our own biased and bloated mindset, structure, and COIN processes.

For a while, U.S. and coalition senior leaders rallied around this program. In 2010, VSO was cited in the Afghan/Pakistan update to President Obama as one of the most impactful COIN initiatives in Afghanistan. This report made the case that senior Taliban and Haqqani leaders were increasingly concerned about VSO as they began to lose control of some of their key territory and safe havens in Regional Commands South and East.[16]

There were other reports as well that cited VSO and ALP success. An article by former Special Operations Task Force Intelligence Officer Andy Feitt stated, "The National Intelligence Estimate of 2011 suggested that VSO and the associated development of Afghan Local Police (ALP) are proving more effective than many other concurrent Coalition military activities."[17]

Going local enhanced interagency cooperation and organizational collaboration.[18] "VSO involved people from USAID, people from State Department, and people from the military working as one unified team," said Zach Harkenrider, State Department Political Military advisor in the U.S. Embassy in Kabul.[19] Zach was another key government civilian who pushed on the diplomatic front in Kabul to achieve local stability. His collaborative approach contributed to many of the key lessons in this framework.

Events like the USSOCOM Academic Week saw multidisciplinary organizations come together in unprecedented numbers. USDA sponsored low-tech agriculture classes for Special Operations Forces. USAID created several economic development programs oriented explicitly around assisting VSO efforts in rural villages. SOF were regular instructors at the Department of State Foreign Service Institute.

It wasn't all rainbows and unicorns — there were still tensions and organizational feuds. But these organizations were playing nicer together and getting more done locally during the VSO period of 2010 to 2013 than in any other period I witnessed in the Afghan war.

Now that we have a holistic understanding of the effects that going local achieved, let's look at how it works with the other tools in the stability toolbox.

About this framework

Violence always has, and always will be, part of the local reality in at-risk areas. When dealing with violent extremism, people must be killed, captured, and detained. The question is to what extent. Let's examine a spectrum of conflict as it pertains to dealing with violent extremism *(see Figure 6-1)*.

On one end of the conflict spectrum is *total war*. Firebombing Dresden, attrition warfare in the Pacific, and nuclear bombs on Japan changed the collective behavior of enemy leaders and nations to our way of thinking. It is an option we retain. At some point, in dealing with

MODERN CONFLICT OPTIONS AGAINST VIOLENT EXTREMISM

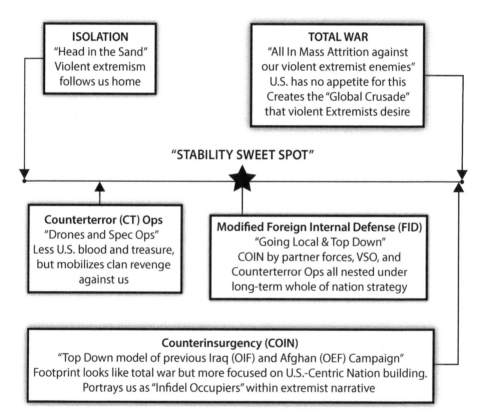

Figure 6-1
The U.S. Spectrum of Conflict in warfare has ranged from isolation to total war. Violent extremism requires a new approach that blends all of these U.S. capabilities within a long –term approach of going local.

violent extremists and their ever-growing propensity for unmitigated violence against us, total war may become a reality for us. But until such time, total war and a strategy of enemy attrition are not in play, based on America's current appetite for this type of violence.

Equally untenable is the other end of the spectrum: doing nothing — *isolationism*. This is pretty much what we've done in Iraq since pulling out, until summer 2014. This is an option similar to the isolationism the U.S. called for after World War I. Many veterans, after multiple combat tours, would like this option as much as our fellow American citizens. But the enemy always gets a vote on the attention he receives from us. And given the extremists' enduring desire to establish a global caliphate, they will likely follow us home, while we're making other plans for minding our own business.

In the middle of the spectrum is *counterinsurgency*. This is the large-footprint, conventional approach we took in Iraq and Afghanistan from 2001 to 2010. It looks a lot like total war, but in reality, it's much more risk-averse, with many more constraints and rules of engagement. It positions our troops and diplomats as contract society–biased occupiers who are trying to manipulate an honor-based status population to accept a Western version of democracy through intrusive top-down stability measures. It's the ineffective 'square tank in a round jirga' model we saw in Chapter 4.

Finally, and closer to the isolation end of the spectrum, are *counterterror operations* through *surgical strikes.* Consider this to be the drone strikes and SOF raids many of us have seen in sound bites on national news. As counterinsurgency fades in popular support, counterterror is becoming preferred as a 'clean' way to keep terror at bay without overly committing our own blood and treasure. It is not as effective, however, as we might think.

"This cutting the head off the snake strategy we've been using since 9/11 is a failed strategy," cautioned retired Lieutenant General Mike Flynn in a recent conference on emerging threats. Flynn gets it; this former Army paratrooper was the director of the Defense Intelligence Agency and intelligence lead for General Stanley McChrystal, who helped build the system for hunting down high-value terror targets after the 9/11 attacks. "Targeted drone strikes make us feel good, but something is not working," he told the assembled crowd of military and law enforcement officers.[20]

But there is something even more ominous about our overreliance on these strikes. There is growing evidence that many of these so-called surgical strikes deep into clan territory, although seemingly innocuous, provoke tribal vengeance in ways that we don't even comprehend yet. Groups like ISIS can harness and mobilize tribal vengeance while living locally among these clans, turning our so-called "surgical strike" efforts against us.

Counterinsurgency and counterterror strikes are effective ways to deal with terror cells, nodes, and leaders. We need to do them. But they are not a singular strategy to win and should be done in the context of a broader approach that systematically renders violent extremists irrelevant locally and globally.

Assuming America is not ready for total war against violent extremists and is looking for a more holistic strategy in which to nest counterinsurgency operations and counterterror operations, there is a better way.

This is the Game Changer "sweet spot" that was applied in Afghanistan and other campaigns from Iraq to Vietnam to Peru. Unfortunately, we allow misguided foreign policy to shelve the best practices that work along with all the stuff that doesn't.

The Game Changer framework in action

This approach is most relevant in areas where violent extremists (or transnational criminals) establish strategic safe havens. They do this by embedding in local communities and exploiting sources of instability that are tied to the gaps between an honor-based clan society and the government — they choose communities that don't have the capacity to handle their own affairs.

There are four primary components of the Game Changer framework (see Figure 6-2). They are:

1. Get surrounded (Village Stability Operations).

2. Meet them where they are.

3. Connect through extreme collaboration.

4. Tell a story that sticks.

Game Changer 1: Get surrounded (Village Stability Operations).

This is the decisive component of the Game Changer framework. Bottom-up and grassroots, this framework is built around the principles of

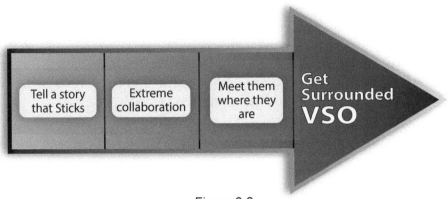

Figure 6-2
Game Changer Framework

Village Stability Operations and connects status society and formal government aspects of contract society. A good example was how the Green Berets in Nagahan Village brought in the Afghan Ministry of Interior to validate the local security force, but only after they helped locals stand on their own.

As we've learned in Afghanistan, VSO alone, however, isn't enough to change the game. We need other enablers.

Game Changer 2: Meet them where they are.

For VSO to work we must accept and work within the local realities. In Nagahan Village, it took two successive teams of Special Forces to identify all the local grievances standing in the way of village autonomy and connection to the Afghan government. Only when these Green Berets and those commanders above them started to empower locals to address their own local problems did they persuade them to stand up for themselves.

Game Changer 3: Connect through extreme collaboration.

It takes more than a village — it takes a network to empower that village. The grievances in Nagahan and other communities were very complex. The organizations capable of helping fractured societies overcome sources of instability were as diverse as the infinite grains of sand in the Kandahar desert. The best way to overcome these extreme challenges — and our own organizational complexities, tensions, and feuding — is with extreme collaboration.

Special Forces in Nagahan reached out across pre-existing networks and organizational seams in order to understand how they should approach stability. By addressing issues like low-tech agriculture and food insecurity through outside experts, Green Berets and their civilian partners made practical changes that worked, improved the lives of the local population, and earned their trust and respect.

Game Changer 4: Lead with story.

Nagahan Village was heavily intimidated. People were frightened to leave their homes. Local development workers wouldn't travel there. The Afghan government and the coalition had written this community off as insurgent controlled. Yet, less than two years after VSO started in this little village, Green Berets helped craft a powerful master narrative of local clans standing up for themselves, supported by their government, against an oppressive and unwanted group of violent extremists. Local Afghans, advisors, and others in their network told compelling stories that brought in other villages asking for VSO expansion to their community.

Finally, local stories amplified into this narrative caused the Afghan Ministry of Interior and the ISAF National Command to choose Nagahan Village as its first ALP validation site in southern Afghanistan. This opened the door for expansion to other areas and congressional funding of ALP. This expansion was possible largely because of a compelling narrative and well-told stories.

A process to make your own

Regardless of where you work in the stability arena — private or public sector, Washington D.C., or a remote village — this framework addresses stability challenges with timeless principles. The key lessons, vignettes, and quotes in the following pages represent some of the most experienced and knowledgeable folks from the vast network of disciplines associated with violent extremism and stability in rough places.[21]

"The bottom-up approach works, but only if you use it. Just talking about it does nothing," says Special Forces team leader Captain Will.

In the following chapters, we will look at the four components of the Game Changers approach in greater depth.

Chapter Highlights

- *Defeating Islamist violent extremists requires that counter-insurgency and counterterrorism be nested within a broader bottom-up stability effort that closes the trust deficits between status and contract society.*

- *The four Game Changer components — (1) get surrounded (VSO); (2) meeting them where they are; (3) connecting and collaborating; and (4) telling a story that sticks — are combined to achieve relative stability and make violent extremists irrelevant to local populations.*

- *VSO and the Game Changer framework go well beyond tribal dynamics and raising militias. They work within the realities of status society for an eventual connection to the state.*

Chapter 7

Getting Surrounded
(Village Stability Operations)

The tyranny of distance

Maiwand District, Kandahar Province, Winter 2010

It was looking grim for the Special Forces detachment's VSO mission in Maiwand District. Malik Jan, the only remaining cooperative, influential elder in Ezabad Village — the designated starting point in the district — had been beaten by the Taliban for collaborating with the Americans. Shortly afterwards, the Special Forces team hit a roadside bomb near his house, sustaining multiple injuries. Afraid, Malik Jan fled to Kandahar City. The team was facing one challenge after the next, and was nearing abort criteria without even having spent the first night in the village.

Villagers told Captain Dan, the team leader, that they would permit his team to enter the village only if they agreed to build a school for them. Dan offered instead to assist them in the project, saying it should come from the village — if his team was allowed to live in the community, and if locals would defend themselves. They refused. Stalemate.

Finally, Captain Dan received reluctant approval to move into the village. Elated, they rented a dilapidated compound on the outskirts of the community that didn't even have a roof. The conditions were so Spartan that only half the team stayed there at a time, while the other half remained on the firebase.

Every week or so, the split detachment would make the perilous journey to conduct resupply and switch out teams. They weathered dozens of attacks by insurgents, and fortunately the team managed to avoid the common roadside bombs. They kept enormous pressure on the insurgents through precision targeting. The reception in the village remained icy.

Despite the ever-present threats, the team stayed laser-focused on moving into the community. Bit by bit, they improved the compound, and before long, there was actually a roof over their heads.

This incremental improvement continued even after a new team replaced Captain Dan's team. Captain John, the new detachment commander, focused his men on continued engagement with the locals. Despite no initial gains, they kept patrolling and stayed committed.

One evening, the team's compound came under enemy fire. The men took up their defensive positions on the roof. Captain John judged the attackers to be too far away for his Green Berets to engage without causing possible civilian casualties. Showing amazing restraint in the face of enemy fire, the team rode out the attack, with no casualties.

The family down the road was not so lucky. The head of the household had been killed in the crossfire by the Taliban. The team appropriately waited for the mourning period to end, and then went to the family bearing traditional gifts of a goat, rice, and beans.

The Green Berets paid their respects to the family in true Afghan fashion and offered condolences. Looking away from Captain John, the slain villager's son said, "You shouldn't apologize, you did not do this." He pointed in the direction the Taliban fire had come from and said, "They did."

This was a significant turning point. There would be many more struggles, but now locals started stepping up to address them. The tyranny of distance that plagued so many COIN practitioners in Maiwand District was much smaller for these Green Berets living among the people in Ezabad.

Captain Dan returned to the same village to build on his initial gains.[1] By the time Dan's team rotated home from their second deployment in this village, Maiwand District had formed an Afghan Local Police force, Malik Jan had returned to Ezabad Village to lead his people, Afghan Special Forces were starting to advise the Afghan Local Police, and the locals had built their own school, providing their own labor and their own teacher.

The Maiwand mission, despite its challenges, offered strategic value to the Afghan campaign and a new opportunity for stability. Most important, this important crossroads on the Silk Road was starting to handle its own affairs again. It would take many years of patient advising, but the seeds for rebuilding informal civil society had been sown.

As difficult as it is, how do we export the success of Maiwand to other rough places? The trick is to identify the ones that meet our strategic goals. This means doing our homework before starting the legwork.

Start small and scale up

First, we need to select the right communities. Maiwand was a very small district with few inhabitants, but it was strategic. It represented significant historical and narrative value to the Afghan people for their stand against the British. To the Taliban, it was a rallying point. For the coalition, its location was critical to commerce.

Second, this is about economy of scale. In baseball, home runs may be more dramatic, but base hits achieve better results overall. Stability is no different. Incremental gains are key.

"Most successful start-up businesses today who make it big, do so by finding a model that works, and then replicating the hell out of it," says Professor Stuart Diamond when he teaches his corporate negotiations model to SOF students.

This is exactly how Afghan VSO went from seven villages in the beginning to dozens of sites in less than two years. But before you can scale up the methodology, you have to fundamentally understand how VSO works in an individual community.

An introduction to Village Stability Operations (VSO)

Remember, VSO was designed for specific conditions. It works in under-governed areas dominated by status societies. These outlying areas, which once handled their own affairs, are now damaged or destroyed. They are now influenced by violent extremists or transnational criminals who seek strategic safe haven to project violence against the U.S.

Relative stability is the overall goal for VSO. For the purposes of this book, we will define Village Stability Operations as *bottom-up and top-down stability actions that connect and restore trust, capacity, and stability between formal governments and informal civil society.*

Basic VSO principles:

1. VSO is bottom-up and top-down.

2. Timing is everything.

3. Getting surrounded is critical, since going local is essential to relative stability.

VSO employs three stability lines of effort: (a) security, (b) economic development, and (c) governance. These are the essential ingredients.

In VSO, these stability ingredients flow from the top and bottom.

Counterinsurgency, by way of contrast, applies these same three stability ingredients top-down only and ignores the bottom. This takes away knowledge of local realities, marginalizes locals, and empowers extremists.

Consider the Maiwand VSO. Captain Dan's men recruited local farmers into a community watch to reduce intimidation. They helped them improve local farming practices to overcome food insecurity, and they addressed the dispute resolution problem by convincing Malik Jan to return from self-imposed exile. None of these were top-down, government programs. Yet each initiative directly solved local grievances and persuaded the community to buy into stability.

Top-down programs are also important, but it's a matter of timing. When the community bought in to the bottom-up approach first, the villages *then* supported connecting to the top-down coalition and government programs.

Now that we know the ingredients, we need to learn the recipe. These steps are known as the VSO methodology. This methodology has never been printed in open publication until now. The steps are critical. They may seem counterintuitive, especially to anyone wedded to traditional counterinsurgency and corporate social responsibility practices abroad. These steps are sequential, but we know in complex environments they will likely experience stops and starts and there will be blurring of lines between the steps.

Step 1: Get surrounded and live among them.

"Living in the village is key to the Village Stability Program. If they need something, they have to be able to come to you, and if you need something you have to be able to go to them," said one Civil Affairs team leader in Kandahar Province.[3]

Living successfully among the people only happens as the result of a team effort involving not only soldiers and advisors but also politicians, senior headquarters leaders, and others at the highest levels — all the way down to the local community leaders.

The minute we engage locals, we put their lives at risk. If they experience retribution, we incur a moral responsibility to help push this retribution back. We should never forget that we are asking locals to assume immense personal risk with VSO.

Building trust through relationships is essential. "It's a very compli-cated mission. And it's very difficult to do. You've got to switch from that kinetic mindset. Instead of looking across a gun sight, you have to look across a handshake," said Captain Rob Williams during his VSO mission in Kandahar Province.

But how do we know when we're actually working within the commu-nity? After seeing hundreds of villages and thousands of data points on this question, I've boiled it down to three criteria:

(1) Advisors are in a position to help defend communities day and night — night is when extremists terrorize locals.

(2) Advisors can responsibly oversee everything they start, includ-ing the behavior of locally armed groups, 24-7.

(3) Community members view advisors as valued guests in their community.

Getting into the community, whether it's in Syria or East L.A., can be extremely challenging. But the effort pays dividends that counterinsur-gency doesn't. Only through local presence, along with legitimacy and credibility, can the true bottom-up work begin.

Step 2: Build a community platform.

When Captain Dan's team received permission to live on the outskirts of Ezabad Village, they could now help the community find self-governance and stability. Stability starts, however, with security.

Local security isn't always an advisor-trained militia. "Security isn't necessarily provided by a cop on every corner. But it can be provided by a motivated populace unwilling to give the Taliban access into their village."[4] Captain Alex lived this mantra. This Green Beret captain con-ducted VSO in one of the roughest areas in south Afghanistan, with only a passive security network. Meanwhile, his small team responded to these threat tips and protected the community until locals stood against threats on their own.

While security is critical, at least two-thirds of this methodology is about economic development and governance. The solutions are mostly local, but it does require persistent communication within our own network to address problems that local advisors and communities can't handle.

Economic development for VSO is also known as participatory com-munity development. Dr. David Ellis, in his work on Building Village

Governance Capacity, states that "Building family and village wealth is the essence of Village Stability Operations."[5] Locals are more likely to stand up for themselves and connect to the government if their collective wealth and station in life is improved.

Due to the importance of the clan or group, participatory development works better in the bottom-up portion of VSO, rather than big expensive development projects. We got this wrong in Afghanistan as we tried to throw big projects at VSO sites. Participatory development is superior because "it empowers local people, creates commitment while positioning locals as stakeholders, mobilizes local resources, helps reduce inequality, provides feedback from the local people, increases efficiency, and helps sustain projects," says Dr. Khan Idris, author of *Jirgas: Pashtun Participatory Governance.*[6]

The main thing here is to identify the *grievances* within the community. These sources of instability will vary from place to place. In urban areas, the source of instability might be unemployment for youth. In Ezabad Village, the team quickly learned that food insecurity was a serious source of instability tied to violent extremist intimidation. As the team dug deeper, they learned that loss of farming knowledge was a root cause of instability.

Governance (as opposed to government) should be revitalized during this bottom-up step. Governance, usually by clan systems, is bottom-up and informal. It fills the large gap that the government cannot. "Afghan civic space is the center of gravity for a popular struggle against insurgents," says Dr. Thomas Barfield. He goes on to say that it is critical to "recognize and strengthen community institutions that deal with decision making, dispute resolution, and consensus building at the village level in rural areas."[7]

Looking deeper at the civil society in these exploited areas, we can see that tribes' thousand-year-old tradition of governance has not only degraded, it has fallen prey to extremists who are exploiting honor-shame societies to pursue revenge on a global level.

Dispute resolution is one of the most important aspects of informal governance in these status areas. There is limited access to arable land, clean water, and food. Resource scarcity, combined with honor-revenge culture, often results in feuds. Unmanaged, these feuds can grow into clan wars and destabilizing violence. The extremists' best terror recruits are pissed-off clan members who consider their honor to be at stake. Dispute resolution calms these dangerous tensions.

Governance equals stability when local, legitimate leadership is in play. Things didn't really turn around in Ezabad Village until Green Berets convinced Malik Jan to return home from his Kandahar refuge. This wasn't easy, considering he had been beaten severely by the Taliban. But when he returned, the community started standing up for itself.

When informal leaders lead their communities, they are less likely to be co-opted to mobilize against the state and our homeland. That's why it's *essential to put relationships before transactions and timelines* when dealing with clan society. Take the time to get this right, and this will serve stability efforts well into the future.

Village stability platform

The outcome of this bottom-up step is called the Village Stability Platform (VSP). This is a strategic node and it is the essential component for connecting previously unreachable areas to the host nation government. Equally important, it is the local node that connects communities to contract society and scales VSO up for expansion to new areas.

Why timing is everything

Many at-risk status areas have a deep distrust of the government. It is simply unrealistic to think that locals will support a government that they have historically distrusted simply because a school is being built or they are visited by a group of senior officials.

Only when marginalized local populations can stand on their own will they entertain the stressful notion of loosely connecting with a formal government they don't trust. Country team members, senior military leaders, and local civilian representatives should not wait for the connection. They should work parallel to the VSO community efforts to ensure that government leaders are ready to receive the eventual outreach from informal leaders. The VSO advisor plans to ultimately walk community leaders back to the connection points within contract society. Will we be ready?

There is only one shot to make this connection. Waiting for the village platform to be established before shaping the environment to connect community and government is too late. A district headquarters or municipal center not ready or willing for the outreach from an already skeptical community spells a catastrophic loss of rapport between all parties.

Step 3: Connect bottom to top.

Closing the gap between top and bottom is the hardest part of the VSO methodology. It's about finding and maintaining a manageable balance between these two very different societies.

Interagency cooperation starts here. Despite historic tensions, the connection of detached communities to the government is vital. This connection, invariably, will be shaky and ugly. But this "organized chaos" is necessary for relative stability and rendering violent extremists irrelevant. "This requires recognition that non-state systems of political authority and decision making have an important role to play in governance and need to be linked with the formal state structure," says Dr. Barfield. "Change requires the participation of local actors in the implementation of a national agenda for security, development, and governance so that they believe they have a stake in the process."[8]

This is why trust, so elusive, is also so critical — and why VSO is so important as its facilitator. The local credibility of embedded advisors will persuade locals to eventually cross trust boundaries. The relationships they establish can open connection corridors between top and bottom that were not there before. Going local can provide access to otherwise unreachable areas. This is true whether we're talking about Syria, Yemen, or even at home in Minneapolis.

VSO has the amazing capacity to walk pissed-off locals back to contract society. They will do this because they trust advisors, not the government. This is often just enough to get stability moving again during bottlenecks. Advisors, if connected to a larger interagency team, can reach up and leverage top-down programs as strategic connectors.

Step 4: Work yourself out of a job.

"If what we do is not sustainable at a local level when we pull the plug and leave here in 2014, these guys are going to go right back to tribal warfare," a Navy SEAL in Panjwaii District told me.[9]

This is one of the greatest challenges in stabilizing fragile areas. A backslide in community stability can erode our credibility and make things worse than when we started. Take a look at Helmand Province in Afghanistan after the Marines withdrew in 2014: within a matter of days, Taliban fighters reoccupied villagers and strongholds they had abandoned years prior when the Marines arrived.

When T.E. Lawrence encouraged advisors to "let Arabs do it tolerably" instead of "us doing it perfectly," this is what he meant. Civil society must build enough community resilience that they can stand on their own.

We tend to have a hard time getting out of our own way on this one. We can't seem to let go and let our partners do the heavy lifting. This is a tricky process.

This step requires expansion and transition. Expansion means the reach of bottom-up efforts into more and more rough areas. This is different from the COIN "ink blot," which projects outward from urban areas; some of these VSO areas may originate in the heart of darkness, surrounded by extremists. This is by design. VSO, which addresses local issues and empowers resilient actors, will usually bring 'walk-ins' from other villages. This can lead to rapid growth, as occurred in Oruzgan Province during 2010–11.

Forcing VSO from the top down in order to hasten expansion is a bad tactic. This is what happened with ALP. Elbowing our way into an Iraqi village or inner-city neighborhood that is not ready for this type of advisory work is ineffective. "Smash-mouth" VSO, as it was sarcastically named by Marine Special Operators who were pressured to open sites that weren't ready in western Afghanistan, is the wrong way to go local. If the Maiwand team had forced its way into the community, it wouldn't have been nearly as successful.

Again, patience, self-restraint, and deep knowledge of the local scenario is critical.

There's a saying: "It takes as long to walk out of the woods as to walk into it." It took a long time to break these societies and it will take a long time to fix them. "It's going to take longer and it's going to be more frustrating," Major Tyler told me as he spoke Pashto with the district governor at the Maiwand District Center. "By encouraging Afghans to take the lead in their transition, they will more likely buy into the process."[10] Transition in a broken civil society like Sudan, rife with violent extremist exploitation, takes just as much patience.

The danger of early success

As we learned when building ALP too quickly, early success can be its own worst enemy. When measurable gains first appear in the form of local security, when enemy activity goes down and people start moving around with some degree of normalcy, it can trigger disconnected leaders, already itching to solve the problem on their watch, to want to pull out too early.

Security success does not equal stability success. A security issue is only a symptom of a deeper ailment — deeper stability problems. If advisors withdraw before economic development and governance grievances are solved, these grievances will simply be re-exploited by extremists. Communities then backslide into chaos. The U.S. will lose credibility, big time.

As even the most casual watcher of the news must know, Iraq is a perfect example of this.

Dealing with the legacy of irregular forces

In transition, the demobilization of irregular local forces is a particularly challenging security issue. Local defenders must be re-integrated into civil society. Just look at the challenges some of our veterans are having when they come back home. These are professional warriors. Imagine it in a place like Afghanistan, where local security forces are farmers and shopkeepers, young men searching desperately for lost honor.

Local defense groups, if not properly managed in transition, can devolve into rogue elements that prey on civil society and destabilize local areas. They can make things worse than when you started. Demobilization of local security forces must be planned for well in advance and then readdressed during transition. This is a part of long-term capacity building, and thus can't be handed off too early.

Afghan Local Police (ALP) is a prime example of a local security problem that was handed off way too soon. ALP focused exclusively on security, while omitting the remaining two-thirds of the stability equation, economic development and governance. The effects of this will be felt negatively in Afghanistan for years to come.

VSO as a strategic tool

We've seen how going local is critical to VSO, but its value in terms of intelligence and information is much more than that. Embedded advisors become strategic assets of distinct value to senior leaders. Advisors gain a local understanding that is impossible to gain from behind the wall of a firebase or embassies. This level of local understanding will directly compete with extremists for legitimacy within the community, but it also enables advisors to identify opportunities for top-down support that would never be identified from the outside. They find connection points to bring top and bottom together when the time is right, and allow them to leverage the relationships they've built for strategic gains.

This can be a powerful tool for senior leaders charged with stability in other countries. VSO then becomes a long-term platform for the U.S. embassy as it pursues the Foreign Internal Defense Strategy for its partner nation. VSO transforms local advisors into strategically relevant advocates for civilian diplomats and development leaders who need to connect with areas they otherwise can't reach. This is a huge return on investment for government organizations disconnected from troubled communities.

An excellent example of how VSO can serve the strategic needs of long-term U.S diplomacy is the current bottom-up and highly collaborative efforts conducted by the U.S. embassy and Civil Affairs teams in the Huallaga Valley of rural Peru.[11]

In the Peruvian highlands once dominated by the Shining Path insurgency, narco-crime is making a comeback. U.S. special operators, civilian stability practitioners, and Civil Affairs staffers working out of the U.S. embassy are helping the Peruvian government and local community leaders to head this off.

Leveraging their previous civilian and military experience with VSO in Afghanistan, these country team members are designing a bottom-up approach uniquely suited for rural Peru. By working locally to identify grievances, empower resilient community leaders, and connect to the government from the bottom, this area is already seeing significant improvements in stability and degradation in criminal capacity. Consider the strategic value of that kind of stability in turbulent nations in our own hemisphere.

Going local with VSO is a powerful game-changing tool around the world and at home. However, as we learned in Afghanistan, this isn't enough. The next critical component is embracing local realities.

Chapter Highlights

- *By understanding the Village Stability methodology at the local level, senior leaders and strategists can scale multiple community platforms for strategic reach.*

- *Timing is everything; bottom-up before top-down; relationships before transactions.*

- *Going local isn't just bottom-up. We should connect top-down efforts to community, grass-roots efforts in order to achieve a balance between contract and status society.*

- *Living among the people is crucial to stabilizing rough places.*

- *As part of working yourself out of a job, train host nation surrogates to go local.*

Chapter 8

Meet Them Where They Are — Embracing Local Realities

"The most consistent road to unhappiness that I know comes from turning a blind eye to reality."

— Patricia Ryan Madson, Improv Wisdom

Mullah Mike

His team called him "Mullah Mike." He was the quintessential Green Beret team leader. He was a Christian, spoke fluent Arabic, and yet he studied the Koran intensely. He spoke of religion openly and honestly with his tribal hosts. He immersed himself in the grievances of the Pashtun tribes in North Kandahar Province. These local challenges were his daily passion while conducting VSO in the most arduous circumstances imaginable.

Mike and his team lived in an Afghan village for nearly a year. Like something out of Kevin Costner's *Dances with Wolves*, their embed site was so austere that most team members lost 25 pounds during the deployment. The Taliban attacked them several times per week. Yet every day, dressed in his beard and local Afghan attire known as a Shalwar Kameez, Mike would lead multiple foot patrols through the surrounding villages.

A Georgia native, he was in his element among the low-tech farming. Mike would stop at every Afghan farm and talk with the locals. Mike and his team knew every family, every shop owner, and every cornfield of this contentious rural area, which was also home to many hardcore Taliban extremists.

"See that guy over there?" Mike said to me one day as we walked beside a wheat field. He pointed to a young man working next to his elderly father in the field. "He's local Taliban. I spoke with his Dad a few weeks ago about persuading his son to come home. Looks like the guy is giving it a shot."

One of the Taliban leaders in the surrounding area was a brutal extremist named Sayed Wali. He was constantly trying to push the Americans out of his area. He and Mullah Mike had plenty of run-ins and gunfights as Mike's team embedded deeper and deeper within the village.

But when it was time for Mike's team to rotate home, a messenger arrived, sent from none other than Sayed Wali. He thanked Mike for the respect and honor he showed the local villagers in the area. Wali sent word to Mike that though they were enemies, he was grateful that Mike respected the culture and the people of this area.

Sound crazy? Not really. Mike met locals where they were, not where he wanted them to be.

Enabling VSO

When you apply VSO like Mullah Mike did in this story, you win over the most skeptical communities and defeat the most hardcore extremists. This is known as connective empathy. This is an essential element of VSO tradecraft. Going local will not work without it.

If we fail to do this, we will act in ways that push key populations away from us and into the waiting arms of the extremists. Our complete withdrawal from Iraq, for instance, hung Sunni sheiks, who had been working with our security forces, out to dry. Many were killed and beaten by ISIS for their support to the U.S.

Our disconnected stability actions also contribute to the extremist narrative of "Islam under attack" and fuel an ongoing clan blood feud against the U.S.

"American Foreign Policy and its current generation of practitioners suffer from an almost complete lack of understanding of the critical concept of feasibility as it relates to statecraft in conflict zones," writes Steve Thomas in his recent article in *Real Clear Defense*.[1] Whether it's East African clan society in Somalia or second-generation Somali clans in Minneapolis, it's critical to understand the local realities of these rough areas.

Embracing local realities

When we talk about local realities, in this context we mean pre-existing stability conditions.[2] Embracing them is not just understanding them, which usually just results in a bunch of people admiring a problem and then doing little about it. Embracing is more comprehensive — it means to appreciate and accept the full context of the local realities and then act within that context.

The steps to local reality

Watch yourself and your companions all the time: hear all that passes, search out what is going on beneath the surface, read their characters, discover their tastes and their weaknesses and keep everything you find out to yourself. Bury yourself in Arab circles, have no interests and no ideas except the work in hand, so that your brain is saturated with one thing only, and you realize your part deeply enough to avoid the little slips that would counteract the painful work of weeks. Your success will be proportioned to the amount of mental effort you devote to it.

— T.E. Lawrence, *27 Articles*

Embracing local realities includes the following steps:

(1) Appreciate the human domain;

(2) Define relative stability;

(3) Identify sources of instability;

(4) Leverage resilient actors;

(5) Identify bottlenecks.

Step 1: Appreciate the human domain.

U.S. Special Operations Command defines the "human domain" as the totality of the physical, cultural, and social environments that influence human behavior in population-centric conflict.[3] This is a fancy way of saying the full spectrum of humanity.

Violent extremists strategically exploit the human domain by mobilizing the Islamic world through story and sensational propaganda. They also embrace local realities. ISIS, for example, regularly exploits Sunni grievances as a minority group and even takes advantage of agricultural grievances.

Assessing the human domain means understanding both the big picture and the local level. As with a dartboard, you start big at regional and national levels, and then work down to a local, "bull's-eye" community level. This is a team sport — the senior leaders who ignore this are usually the ones who screw up the policy design or strategic implementation.

Ethnicity and groups

Every at-risk area has a complex and unique human domain. Understanding ethnicities, groups, and group dynamics is a major part of this first step.

In status societies exploited by extremists, group tensions run very deep. These group dynamics help us understand potential flash points for large-scale violence and critical vulnerabilities.

This is much bigger than ethnicity. There are all kinds of group dynamics to consider: There are informal groups such as patronage networks (think old-school crony politics), religious networks, and mujahedeen. There are criminal organizations and even labor unions that influence local issues. Every organization from the U.S. State Department to the tactical military task force should analyze and share this holistic human domain information.

Unfortunately, there isn't much of this happening today.

When assessing these groups along ethnic, tribal, and other lines, consider Dr. Weiner's *The Rule of the Clan*, discussed in Chapter 3. Honor, hospitality, revenge, feud, and other clan codes are universal realities. How do clans affect the local population? How do they affect us? Do they have blood feuds against the U.S. that we should be aware of? How do they typically resolve disputes? How do they go to war? Will our 'surgical strike actions' invoke honor-based revenge against us?

There is also the roles and conflicts of status and contract society. The fact that there are distinct differences between status and contract society will help identify tension points, sources of instability, and — eventually — opportunities to render violent extremists irrelevant.

The discovery process should never stop. When we demonstrate knowledge and empathy for local conditions, we gain credibility and relevance in the eyes of the people who matter most — the locals. The more we do this, the better our sense of clarity as to what stability should actually look like.

Step 2: Define relative stability.

Dr. Seth Jones and the small Special Operations staff who led the initial effort to go local did something in 2009 that had not been done the entire decade of the Afghan campaign — they accurately defined relative stability in Afghanistan. They looked back and identified the most recent period of relative Afghan stability in modern history. The period chosen was the Afghan Musahiban Dynasty (1929–78).

Relative stability is the key here. This was not stability as we know it in the West. It emphasized governance at informal levels where the government couldn't reach. It fell short of the Western stability ideals we projected onto the Afghan people. Though ugly by Western standards, this model was sufficient to deny safe haven to violent extremists, which was our strategic aim point. This model of relative stability became the baseline for the VSO program. It's why locals intuitively 'got it' and supported it.

No matter what area we choose to work in across the globe, we should first develop a comprehensive vision of relative stability that is shared across all policy and command levels. Without a shared vision of relative stability, we can't make strategic choices that are effective or tell a coherent story to the people and groups who matter most.

A lack of consensus on relative stability can also lead to a flawed campaign design, law enforcement approach, foreign business venture or stability mission. A glaring example is the U.S. government–centric policy in Afghanistan, a country where the central government is not a viable singular solution for stability. What if there were a shared definition of relative stability between the Afghan president and the U.S. president, all the way down to Mullah Mike in his remote village post? Would we not have a much better chance at meeting our goals in Afghanistan? This doesn't have to be a mystery. There is a way to do this.

Why relative stability is important

Here is a simple way we can identify relative stability in different places. Ask, "Within recent history (100 years or so), what were the best examples of relative stability in this area that meet our working definition?" Once identified, the period can be pulled apart and analyzed to find out what worked in security, economic development, and governance.

Doesn't it make more sense to start with a baseline understanding of what worked in these areas? Shouldn't history instruct what was palatable to local people, and then see if it meets our goal of creating an environment inhospitable to global extremists? Others are already taking this approach.

Dr. Akbar Ahmed, for example, wrote a book called *The Thistle and the Drone: How America's War on Terror Became a Global War on Tribal Islam*. In it, he describes the 'Waziristan Model.' This is the best model I've seen to describe the breakdown and exploitation of clan society by violent extremists. One of the main points in Dr. Ahmed's book is that the top-down Global War on Terror approach of drone strikes and raids is very ineffective and actually spawns tribal violence against the U.S. To make this point, Ahmed painstakingly explains Pashtun tribal society in the wild western frontier of Waziristan before violent extremism took over. He uses relative stability — past, present, future — to present his argument.

Ahmed admits that the former historical model is likely too far gone to restore today, but by understanding what relative stability once looked like, we have a much better chance of finding locally appropriate solutions.[4]

The first step is to examine the top-down actions of contract society. What were the formal actions of the government in our target area to assert control over its territory through force, programs, or services? How did the government provide these functions down to the outlying areas? Where did it fall short?

The contract society shortfalls will show us how clan society filled the gap. This is the bottom-up research that's often overlooked because of our Western top-down bias. We should ask ourselves, "What were the clan, tribal, and other grass-roots systems that provided relative stability at local levels?"

Once we understand the relative stability model of the past, we have to also understand relative stability today. Now we can leverage our historic definition of stability to inform our current assessment. This gives us a baseline understanding of where things stand now.

With this baseline capacity definition of past and current relative stability, we're now ready to define a strategic goal that is rooted in local relevance.

What should the way forward look like in relation to status and contract society? Where should these two societies connect? Where should they not? How we define relative stability as our strategic aim point becomes the overall focus point for how we go local.

Once these questions are answered, we need to share this definition broadly across our interagency and organizational networks.

If we do this right, it will help keep us from employing poorly managed local militia programs for short-term gains while creating long-term liabilities, as we have attempted in Syria.

An important caveat: Sharing a perspective of relative stability will fail if all stakeholders are not involved in framing these realities from the outset. It is very important to be inclusive. We can only see one piece of the pie, so we must bring in other stakeholders with equal or more relevant perspectives on the problem if we are to gain true understanding of what's really going on in these places. This collaborative problem framing takes a little more effort, but is pure gold when facing complex stability issues.

Step 3: Identify sources of instability.

Syria, as I write this, is a huge problem in the Middle East. Almost every U.S. government organization that has an interest in Syria is focused on the security situation. As we should have learned in Afghanistan and Iraq, the real problems come in after the tin-pot dictator is overthrown or the pipeline is installed and the village displaced. Once the dust clears, people's simmering expectations for change in these fragile areas start to boil over. These expectations become sources of instability. Our use of them will determine whether they are liabilities or assets to our strategic outcomes.

Sources of instability are social grievances that lead local people to fight or flee. They are magnets to violent extremists seeking relevance in local areas. ISIS will exploit sectarian rifts between Sunni and Shi'a in Iraq, just as al Qa'ida will exploit Afghan tensions between Pashtun tribes. The terror group al Shabaab will provoke fights between clans over land control that might reach back to Somali diasporas in the U.S.

Largely because of our contract society–biased behavior, these social issues don't attract our attention, but they could — and they must if we are going to defeat violent extremists. These sources of instability represent tremendous opportunity. The reality is that locals are often more connected to their status societal systems than extremists think.

Because identifying sources of instability is immensely challenging, starting early, with deep preparation, is very important. However, the process never stops. Mullah Mike identified most of the sources of instability in his village only after he lost his first 10 pounds from eating rice and lamb every day while living among the Alikozai tribe.

Step 4: Identify resilient actors.

Just knowing what destabilizes an area isn't enough, however. We need to find locals who can address these issues.

"For moral reasons, but also for practical ones, indigenous peoples must be made primary stakeholders in nation-building efforts," explains John C. Hulsman. "Working with leaders with genuine local legitimacy is central to the process, and above all the West should help but not dictate, facilitate, but not dominate, influence but not run, advise but not manage.... For Lawrence it was self-evident that failing this, nation-building efforts would not prove self-sustaining."[5]

"We need local solutions for local problems," Green Beret Captain Rob told me in a Kandahar interview. Rob met with tribal elders in his area every day. In persistent relationship-building discussions and interactions with locals, he started to identify actors with potential solutions that weren't visible when his team was driving in and out of these areas.

We call them resilient actors.

Dr. Howard Clark, Marine, USAID Field Representative and intelligence professional, defines a resilient actor as "a person or network that strengthens societal capacity while opposing violent extremists." Simply put, a resilient actor is someone who is local, legitimate, and a positive contributor to our definition of relative stability.

Resilient actors can be either an antibody or accelerant to violent extremism. Many times, which course they take is based on our behavior — especially if we dishonor them or marginalize them. This is true at home, and abroad.

Once again, our Western biases get in the way here. These resilient actors are often different from government leaders. Many times they belong to informal, lesser-known networks that may not be apparent to us unless we are really paying attention. We can unintentionally push away some of the most relevant resilient actors, while promoting government leaders who actually are destabilizing figures.

Resilient actors are sometimes not the ideal choices as partners by traditional Western diplomacy standards. They want to simply protect their traditional way of life from any outside interference. They may dislike us, especially at first, as much or more as they dislike external violent extremists, and that's okay. These types of relationships take time. What matters is that we come to realize how vital these informal leaders are to relative stability, and develop the capacity to find and cultivate these important relationships. It's harder than we might think, especially when they don't want to be found.

Resilient actors are frequently targets for intimidation and retribution. They are intimidated, beaten, and even killed by extremists. In other areas, they are marginalized and overshadowed by a new breed of armed power broker, like ISIS. No wonder these leaders often slip quietly into the shadows.

For these reasons, finding resilient actors isn't easy. They hide from intimidation. They use surrogates. They leave their community in favor of safer areas. Or they simply 'check out' from frustration — often from watching our uninformed support of corrupt local leaders who prey on the community. Bringing them back into the sunlight of leadership takes tradecraft and a process.

One thing is certain — we sure as hell can't find them by launching drone strikes and SOF raids into their communities as our only strategy.

"Finding the true elders and leaders of the villages is probably the most difficult thing you are going to encounter when you move to a VSO site," Captain Jeremy Schwendeman explained from his embedded village site in 2010.[6]

"The village elder is not necessarily the first guy with a white beard that comes up to your patrol with his hand out," said Green Beret Captain Rob.

In one Kandahar village where SOF were going local, they completely overlooked the true resilient leaders for a year!

Relevant resilient leaders will change over time. Some will be excellent at stabilizing local communities for security. Others will be naturally suited for dispute resolution. Some will exist in the shadows and will require coaching and mentorship. In many areas, these connections to the government are so strained and violence so rampant that very few community leaders have the experience or willingness to make these connections. Once again, this takes time, but it starts by finding them.

Step 5: Identify bottlenecks.

Bottlenecks are clogged social conditions in civil society that are preventing resilient actors from addressing sources of instability.

Learning why community leaders aren't solving local problems — whether it's due to extremist intimidation, lack of will or capacity, or our own self-inflicted actions — will provide us with critical insights to the bottom-up approach needed to achieve relative stability in these rough places. Since bottlenecks occur throughout status and contract society, it takes leaders at all levels to collaborate on finding these blockages to stability. It's often beyond the limited purview of the advisor living in a community to identify the bottleneck, but it's also probably kicking his ass the most. This is a major reason why network collaboration on all levels is so important.

An unfortunate success metric

When we find the locals who can overcome these sources of instability, we are threatening the relevance of extremists. Bad actors get fear in their eyes at this point. Resilient actors will start getting blown up. They will be kidnapped. They will be publicly beaten. If we prepare for this reality, work to protect resilient actors, and remain persistent, the intimidation will subside as resilient actors continue to gain relevance.

Some enemy pushback is more nuanced than outright violence. Extremists, for example, will also use their own networks with politicians, the press, and social media to spin a detrimental narrative against going local.

Anonymous and well-connected callers will escalate reports of human rights violations committed by community defenders. Some of these reports will be valid, but most others will be extremist misinformation. How we respond to these false narratives is critical. As we'll learn in Chapter 10, without a coherent campaign design that supports bottom-up governance and a master narrative that communicates it, this is where going local will fail.

The art of embracing local realities

There is more than process to this approach: there is also mindset. There must be a desire to embrace local realities as if we were learning about our own ancestral history. Anything less than a deep understanding will keep us on the sidelines while extremists run circles around us in a game we don't understand.

Be self-aware and keep an open mind. So much of this runs counter to our traditional sensibilities. Self-awareness reduces Western biases in local situations. An open mind reminds us that uncomfortable solutions can still lead to relative stability. Some stability options may be downright distasteful. But if they render the environment inhospitable to extremists, they bear consideration.

First, do no harm. This code of conduct for doctors applies to leaders at all levels. Every intervention can cause unintended negative effects. The massive Afghan war economy is an example of senior leaders failing to embrace local realities. In Syria, almost no one is talking about drought and tribal tensions, but they sure will be when the dust clears and we find ourselves occupying these places.

Understand status versus contract society. Understanding the fundamental principles of these two worlds is key for every policymaker, statesman, development expert, and warrior. We often unconsciously devalue status society. This makes us much less legitimate in local areas, while increasing extremist legitimacy. Mark Weiner's *The Rule of the Clan* and Jared Diamond's *The World Until Yesterday* are essential primers for reaching this understanding.

Think broader than security. Our tendency is to analyze the enemy only. We ignore the other critical elements of civil society. This gives violent extremists opportunities to fill the stability gaps that we leave open, and entrench their relevance. Lieutenant General Michael Flynn's paper *Fixing Intel* is one of the most comprehensive works to date on this subject.[7]

For instance: Social network mapping of indigenous civil society is a critical tool set for going local, and yet our broader intelligence focus often ignores this. Social network mapping presents leaders with more options for collaboration and natural antibodies to extremism.

Without it, we miss all manner of bottom-up solutions for stability. Broader intelligence focus happens when policymakers, strategists, commanders, and practitioners require more from intelligence than identifying threat networks.

Tradecraft for VSO

This is more than just understanding grievances. It is critical for us to act, but to act responsibly, thoughtfully, and effectively. Embracing local realities will make our actions more locally appropriate, even if the correct action is to do nothing.

Embracing local reality, however, isn't a solo endeavor. It requires knowledge that many advisors don't have. It requires working with specialized subject matter experts that exist in a parallel, but compartmentalized universe from security forces, advisors, and practitioners. We have to bring them all together in a cohesive tribe. To embrace local realities, it takes more than a village...it takes a network. And that is the focus of our next chapter.

Chapter Highlights

- *At a minimum, embracing local realities means identifying the human domain, relative stability, sources of instability, resilient actors, and bottlenecks.*

- *Understanding the human domain identifies relevant actors, groups, and networks. It shows the tensions and opportunities within them.*

- *Relative stability is a balance between status and contract society that is inhospitable to violent extremists.*

- *Defining relative stability creates a shared goal for success that is supportive of our strategic needs, locally appropriate and achievable.*

- *When we understand sources of instability, we understand what locals care most about and what extremists are exploiting. They also show us the opportunity for our local action.*

- *Resilient actors are legitimate local leaders and networks that can overcome sources of instability.*

- *Bottlenecks are social clogs that must be addressed to restore stability.*

Chapter 9

Extreme Collaboration:
It Takes a Village and a Network

*"Where everyone is connected, the game-changer is col-
laboration. Reaching across boundaries, often abetted by
technology that connects us all, collaboration unleashes
the power of the many to do together what none can do
alone."*

— William Bratton and Zachary Tumin,
Collaborate or Perish

USSOCOM Headquarters, Tampa, Florida, February 2011

"We have to change the way we prepare for Afghanistan."

Special Forces Major Ed paused and looked intensely around the room of assembled junior leaders in the Special Operations Command Headquarters.

Ed was an up-and-coming Green Beret officer from Third Special Forces Group and one of the original architects of VSO in eastern Afghanistan. He was a visionary and one of the most respected officers across all the Special Operations units.

"VSO is growing faster than any of us expected. Since we started living in the villages our guys are facing all kinds of new challenges. Our current pre-deployment preparation doesn't fit into our operational reality at all, especially since we hardly know each other when we get there."

"Just look around the room. We've been at this for nearly a decade and we are still showing up to Afghanistan as a Special Operations pick-up team."

I liked Ed's analogy. A pick-up team is just fine for a Saturday afternoon basketball game, but not for a joint force deployment to go local into some of the most complex and adverse societies in the world. In this upcoming deployment, West Coast Navy SEALS would combine with

East Coast Marines and Green Berets to live and work in rural villages on life-or-death missions — but they had never trained together.

"It's more than just joint military shortfalls," he continued. "Interagency cooperation is even worse. Department of State, USAID, Department of Agriculture, and CIA are all working in the same remote places we are. We need them and they need us. Yet we don't see them at all in our pre-mission training. It doesn't make any sense."

Heads around the room were nodding in unison. Everyone had seen these problems and knew of the gaps in pre-mission training.

"The problems we face on the ground are very complex. Our guys are living in villages where they have to deal with Afghan social grievances that the Taliban are exploiting, like farming shortfalls, tribal disputes, and water shortages. But all of our pre-deployment training is based on lethal combat tasks of shooting, moving, and communicating — not identifying and addressing local problems that are kicking our ass."

"So, what do you suggest," a young SEAL lieutenant asked.

Ed looked squarely at him before he spoke. "We need a pre-mission training event that prepares our operators for the demands of VSO. And it needs to happen at the very beginning of the deployment cycle, so that we have time to go deeper on our knowledge gaps."

I noticed a lot of head nodding and affirmative grumbling at this point. Ed swung his gaze to me, and with an ever so slight smile asked, "So, Lieutenant Colonel Mann, does this sound like something you and SOCOM could put together for us?"

As every head in the room turned to look at me, I realized that I had just walked headlong into a masterful ambush set up by my old buddy Ed.

"Yes, I think we can," I said with more confidence than I was feeling, especially since I hadn't even informed headquarters of what I'd signed us on for.

But Ed knew I wanted to see this kind of event happen. And building momentum for this at the grass-roots level was the only chance we had.

And with that, USSOCOM Academic Week was born. Less than seven months later, in an old middle school gym on Fort Bragg, North Carolina, nearly 700 Navy SEALs, Marines, and Green Berets showed up for this one-of-a-kind training initiative. This five-day academic stability event consisted of three campuses and 21 classes that included topics like tribal dynamics, economic development, and best-practice panels of special operators who had just returned from the VSO mission.

This was a training audience for the folks doing the heavy lifting. Junior officers, sergeants, and civilian practitioners charged with going local in Afghanistan. General Petraeus kicked off the training via video teleconference from Afghanistan, followed by the U.S. Ambassador to Afghanistan. A four-star Army general and the most senior U.S. civilian in Afghanistan were addressing an audience of junior officers and sergeants on what their mission would be. Not bad for a bottom-up fueled training event.

Although the trainees were implementers, the event was supported by very senior leaders. This included the commander of USSOCOM, general officers, Congressional staffers, and senior executives from USAID and U.S. Department of Agriculture. Far beyond merely the Department of Defense, there were over 30 instructors who ranged from Special Operations, USAID, the U.S. Department of Agriculture, nongovernmental organizations, and even leaders from the Afghan government.

SOCOM Academic Week became a powerful training event not just for Special Operations Forces, but also for conventional forces and civilians preparing for Afghanistan. "Academic Week offered up an extensive curriculum on the methodology they developed for local police and village stability as well as a rich menu of Afghan, Pashtun, and Islamic expertise with native speakers, experts, retired intelligence officers, and returning operators," Linda Robinson pointed out in her book *One Hundred Victories*.[1]

This was a substantive change in how we prepared for going local.

For two years, every six-month training cycle to Afghanistan now began with this collaborative, multidisciplinary academic course. For the first time in over a decade of war, SEALS, Green Berets, and Marines came together, trained, and knew each other before they hit the battlefield.

Interagency members from alphabet organizations like USAID and the U.S. Department of Agriculture not only attended Academic Week, they were instructors. They reciprocated by inviting SOF to teach in their institutions. I was invited to explain our approach of going local to diplomats at the Foreign Service Institute multiple times. Most importantly, over 2,500 SOF and stability practitioners were trained in these discrete yet vital stability topics. Many told me later the training saved lives and dramatically improved mission performance.

What is even more significant is not what Academic Week produced, but how it occurred, because it's a core Game Changer issue: This event didn't come from senior levels on high — a visionary young major and a handful of believers initiated it in a corner planning room.

If you remember anything from this chapter, remember this:

In post–9/11 conflicts, leaders at even the most junior levels can foster strategic change like never before. Academic Week is but one example of how a grassroots effort connected to a network can achieve strategic effects.

The game changer no one knows about

While most people are familiar with VSO and Afghan Local Police, very few know about the Game Changer that enabled this bottom-up program to become a strategic national program: collaboration. Just as USSO-COM Academic Week evolved from collaboration, so too did VSO. It's just plain essential in our modern, complex, ever-changing world. Used in concert with going local, it can achieve remarkable outcomes.

A growing movement

"In the digital world, decentralization will continue to change the face of industry and society. Fighting these forces of change is at best futile and at worst, counterproductive."

— Ori Brafman and Rod A. Beckstrom,
The Starfish and the Spider

There is growing consensus across our community endorsing collaboration as a best practice to solve hard problems. "Organizations that collaborate are much more viciously competitive than those who don't," says Professor Stuart Diamond. "Organizations who collaborate generate four times as much value as those who don't."[2] This is especially true in security and stability.

Admiral William McRaven, Commander of U.S. Special Operations Command, said this in his guidance to Special Operations Forces: "Imagine 2020, a time when joint, interagency, intergovernmental, multinational, nongovernmental, commercial, and academic partners cooperate, trust each other, and combine their capabilities and authorities to provide National Leadership with strategic options. Times such as these can originate only from unprecedented levels of mutual trust, confidence, and understanding that recognize no fixed boundaries and foster networking and collaboration."

Collaboration in the private sector can increase profits and reduce risk. But in dealing with stability issues, it can save lives and win wars.

Dr. Dave Warner, a collaboration pioneer, dubbed this approach "radical inclusion." Dr. Warner claimed that the most valuable information in a conflict or disaster zone was information that could be shared with everybody."[3] Professor Diamond refers to it as "aggressive collaboration." There are lots of terms, but for our high-stakes environment, I'll call it extreme collaboration. Let's look closer at what this means to us.

As budgets get tighter, we are mired in endless bureaucratic red tape and organizational squabbling. Knowledge gaps, isolation, and process quickly become our detractors. Let's look at each of these internal issues a little more closely.

1. Knowledge gaps. If you're a local advisor or stability practitioner, you'll be working among people who face wicked stability problems that far exceed your organic capacity to define, much less overcome. "Wicked," in this case, doesn't mean evil, but rather immensely complex. A wicked problem is an unstructured, tangled mess of social conditions. Every wicked problem is unique, as well as interactively complex. They include problems we saw in degraded Afghan villages such as food insecurity, tribal tensions, and damaged dispute resolution capacity.

Wicked problems usually exceed the capacity of the average civilian advisor, soldier, or law enforcement officer working in local areas. Many of these problems are so complex they require diverse experts to work together. This is a challenge for several reasons, mainly due to isolation and ineffective process.

2. Isolation. Isolation usually occurs geographically with local advisors working in remote locations. However, isolation also applies to any relevant party, from policy to tactical levels, who is isolated within the vast stability network, and can't get beyond his own email address list or operational reporting chain. This organizational flaw leaves numerous talented individuals on the periphery of the local advisor's universe even though many of them are desperately seeking to connect.

Isolation can prevent leaders and advisors from connecting to the people and organizations that can address these glaring problems. It prevents communication in every direction. Our own stability network is so socially complex that we have a very hard time finding the right person or group that can actually assist with the local problem.

3. Antiquated process. Whether it is private sector or government work, we still use the same outdated, layered chain-of-command process we used throughout the 20th century to solve structured problems, and do the bare minimum of work with outside organizations. This antiquated process discourages cooperation. Cooperation is an afterthought or a last resort.

John F. Schmitt writes, "Many of these situations cross institutional boundaries, so that even if commanders have the necessary comprehension, they lack the authority to act unilaterally. Any solutions or methods they adopt must satisfy various groups of stakeholders."[4] Wicked problems bleed over into the proprietary domain of other organizations. Bureaucratic clan warfare is usually the result.

Reaching across organizational seams is often taboo. Working with other organizations is usually reserved for senior leaders or is tightly controlled from the top. In this hyper-connected world, where we still fight over budgetary and jurisdictional rice bowls, it's a major reason why extremist groups are selling tens of thousands of ISIS T-shirts to kids around the world, while the State Department counterterror website languishes behind.

There are similar problems in higher levels. If you're a senior leader in a foreign capital city, a CEO in a corporate headquarters, or even a policymaker back in Washington, D.C., many of your strategic problems emanate from local areas you can't reach and don't understand. For example, the terror group ISIS mobilizes support from pissed-off Sunni tribes who are excluded from the Shia-dominated Iraqi government. Senior leaders have no real access into those turbulent places. Yet these Sunni tribal areas are centers of gravity to the extremists who are giving us fits.

Because today's stability problems are more unstructured and our networks are more convoluted than ever, our collective inefficiencies are just as damning to stability as violent extremism.

This is why we need extreme collaboration. Most people with relevant technical knowhow find it hard to get into these violent areas. Those who do usually are gunslingers — not hydrologists or economic development experts.

Some people, usually more in the private sector, are collaborating on all sorts of complex issues, at an amazing pace. People from diverse backgrounds and cultures swarm on wicked problems from every corner of the globe. They do this every day to enhance their financial bottom line and improve efficiency.

This is the new world we live in. It's time to shed antiquated procedures and get in the flow of proven processes that will carry us through the complex, murky waters of stability and allow us to outpace violent extremists.

The process is extreme collaboration.

What it means to us

Collaboration has several distinct advantages in overcoming wicked stability problems and our internal organizational complexity.

1. *Extreme collaboration helps us understand the problem better.* Today's stability problems are so wicked we have trouble accurately framing the problem down to root causes of instability. In many unstable areas, the answers to these complex problems are a mystery buried by the sands of enduring conflict and intimidation. Leveraging the shovels of multiple organizations, such as economic development and governance organizations, uncovers much more about the problem and reveals a much broader understanding of what still lies beneath the surface.

2. *Extreme collaboration brings powerful solutions to bear.* Private sector and government stakeholders bring many sources of knowledge, talent, and resources.

"With development and governance, you have to flatten out relationships a bit," said the Green Beret lieutenant colonel I'll call John. He was the Village Stability Coordination Center Director in Regional Command South, where interagency coordination with Department of State and USAID was a daily necessity.[5] This flattening of relationships, if done consistently, will quickly outpace traditional stovepiped methods. As these multidisciplinary relationships thicken, it can also lead to a very potent effect called swarming.

"Swarming is a seemingly amorphous, but deliberately structured, coordinated, strategic way to perform military strikes from all directions," says John Arquilla and David Ronfelt of RAND.[6] This military-based definition also describes how combining the talents of diverse stability actors can achieve similar effects on complex social problems and violent extremists.

3. *Extreme collaboration allows us to play to our strengths in spite of wicked problems.* We need each other. For example, ISIS continues to brutally target civilians who are trying to help degraded communities. These collaborative and diverse connections with special operators, soldiers, and law enforcement personnel who can create space for the civilian stability expert will become very important. We should start building this collaborative process now. The relationship between the nonprofit Spirit of America and U.S. Special Operations working in at-risk areas abroad is a good case study for this.

Spirit of America is a nonprofit organization committed to supporting our military and diplomats as they stabilize rough areas. They bring donors and skills that security forces just don't have to address wicked, local problems. Gunslingers and advisors need the skills and experience of outside stability organizations like Spirit of America and the vast network they bring to the table. "The problems encountered by U.S. troops and diplomats often require private sector skills (such as business creation) and resources beyond those available through government channels,"[7] says CEO and founder Jim Hake of the Los Angeles–based organization.

4. *Extreme collaboration closes the knowledge and communication gap between contract and status society.* In a bottom-up environment, senior leaders require local perspective to make informed decisions and to communicate reality to their bosses and constituents back home. Conversely, local advisors and stability practitioners need the context, resources and authorities of senior leaders when encountering stability 'bottlenecks' in their local areas. This is new.

Building strategic design around local realities flies in the face of conventional military hierarchy and chain-of-command communication. It requires unprecedented compression of command lines into a "flat" architecture. For example, General Petraeus, the former ISAF commander, addressing in-bound captains and sergeants at Academic Week was unprecedented for military protocol, but it set an important precedent for future "flat" communications between advisors in villages and this NATO commander. These strategic-to-tactical real-time sessions continued, and had significant impact on VSO becoming a strategic program supported by Congressional funding.

5. *Extreme collaboration reduces transaction costs.* Collaboration finds the right people, at the right time, to solve the right problem. This is a huge strategic return on investment when working in complex and ambiguous environments. Otherwise, discovery learning and bumbling

through efforts to find answers and assets, while in high-stakes conditions, drains us of precious blood and treasure.[8]

Collaboration in action

Extreme collaboration really is the secret sauce to achieving grand effects in an age of complexity. For my money, no one has created a better collaboration framework than Ori Brafman and Rod A. Beckstrom in their book, *The Starfish and the Spider: The Unstoppable Power of Leaderless Organizations*.[9]

Brafman and Beckstrom use exhaustive research and examples to show how hierarchical organizations (spiders) are being overcome by collaborative, decentralized organizations (starfish) in the complex new age. Their "five legs of the starfish" model is excellent for understanding collaboration.

With some modifications, here is how this collaboration model works for stability.

1. Stability tribes

Seth Godin, one of the most innovative marketers and collaborative thinkers of our age, has called today's collaborative circles tribes.[10] These tribes are not the traditional clans and families from remote geographic areas, but rather informal groups of people who share common beliefs and ideology or concern for a common problem. I'll call them stability tribes.

In many tribal areas around the world, when locals get together to solve problems, they sit in a circle. The circle itself is significant. There is no first among equals within this circle, as it represents leaders from various groups who come together whenever a problem arises. Like with the Round Table of King Arthur's court, everyone in this circle has a voice. The circle convenes only when a problem arises. It dissolves when solutions are rendered. The concept of problem-solving circles plays out time and again in clan societies. Today's problems require this old-school approach.

The concern for a common problem is what presents unprecedented opportunity to overcome organizational parochialism and work together. These modern, multidisciplinary tribes are the collaborative problem-solving body for the game changer framework. We should consider them in every game changer component.

Stability tribes are usually very inclusive. I've seen them form from diverse backgrounds around problems ranging from agriculture to strategic messaging. They include people from policy and strategic levels all the way down to local villages. Tribes are very inclusive of academia, special operations, government, and the private sector as long as they are relevant to the problem at hand.

Even though many of these network tribes are virtual, you will often find a sense of community and problem ownership. In fact, tribes that are aligned in purpose for solving a common problem are often very useful in overcoming pre-existing tensions between disparate organizations. What tensions?

Group rivalry isn't just reserved for status society. The U.S. and our allied governments, along with many nongovernmental organizations, exhibit just as many emotional tendencies of honor and revenge as any ancient status society.

The fact is, we are still much more status society than contract, no matter how advanced we think we might be. Does that surprise you?

While modern humans appeared around 200,000 years ago, our contract society traits, such as rule of law and individualism, are quite recent. With agriculture only arriving 10,000 years ago and nation states less than 6,000 years ago, "all human societies have been traditional for far longer than any society has been modern," says Jared Diamond.[11]

That's why your spouse, when pissed at you, doesn't care anything about your logical explanations for why you acted the way you did. She won't hear anything from you until she feels there is connective empathy on your part and that you 'get where she is coming from.' That is basic clan behavior based on emotion, honor, and atonement. It's no different from an advisor atoning for collateral damage to a village elder or rival clansman publicly atoning for a wrong committed against another clan in order to prevent a blood feud.

We exhibit all manner of clan behavior in contract society without even realizing it. From the boardroom to the tearoom, clan behavior still flows through our veins, especially when we become emotional, or when the stakes are high. Therefore, if we want a distinct edge in human connections and building tribes across organizational seams, we should go old school and embrace status and contract societies as if they were part of a single iceberg *(see Figure 9-1)*.

We are all more status society than we realize, especially in high-stakes, emotional situations. The primary elements of status society lurk

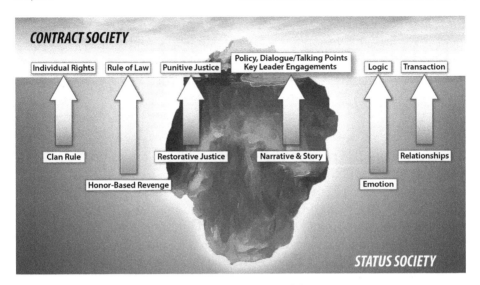

Figure 9-1. The Iceberg of Society
We are all more status society than we realize, especially in high-stakes, emotional situations. The primary elements of status society lurk beneath the surface but directly inform our contract society actions. Honor, for example, often trumps logic. And transactions greatly depend upon relationships, no matter how sweet the deal. Our enduring biological connection to status society is also why interagency rivalries often look a lot less like collaborative disagreements and more like feuds between the Hatfields and McCoys.

beneath the surface but directly inform our contract society actions. If human perception is an iceberg, it's below the surface where our deepest connections and our greatest potential for extreme collaboration reside.

When looking at this iceberg, our understanding of the status society components below the surface directly inform those contract society tendencies that we see on the surface in our everyday life. For example, State Department leaders and other U.S. military groups with proprietary concern about local activities will often respond more favorably to supporting your mission when relationships precede transactions. Similarly, a Congressman considering whether or not to fund your mission will be more receptive to a PowerPoint presentation that is informed by a well-told story than dry bullet points.

Like traditional tribal councils, stability tribes are not permanent. They ebb and flow. They can form quickly around a discrete stability problem, work together to illuminate the problem, frame it for action, develop a collaborative way ahead, and then recede once the problem is addressed. When we identified the need for Academic Week, we formed a tribe that consisted of SEALS, Green Berets, Marines, USAID, the U.S. Department of Agriculture, various academic institutions, and nonprofit groups, just to name a few.

However, once the stability tribe is formed, we need a champion.

2. Champions

The best grass-roots collaboration in the world won't accomplish a damn thing without resources and support. For that, you need horsepower. Enter the champion. They are not just normal leaders; they are leaders with influence, power, resources, knowledge, and authority, who are passionate for a common cause. They understand and embrace their role, which ranges from providing top-cover to serving as 'Cheerleader-in-Chief' to organizations formed from tribes that don't historically play well together.

During SOCOM Academic Week our champion was Admiral McRaven, the legendary SOF Commander who oversaw the effort to kill Osama bin Laden. McRaven saw the utility in the training event from the outset. He funded it and sponsored it. He cleared a path for our efforts by bulldozing all traditionalist naysayers out of the way.

Champions are also CEOs for big corporations, mayors, and police chiefs. They can be athletes, movie stars, and writers. Author Steven Pressfield was a huge champion for Green Beret Jim Gant's One-Tribe-at-a-Time concept. Champions lend 'star power' to movements and give them strategic energy. For this reason, they are the ones often remembered for big movements — and they should be.

Champions are not afraid to take a stand and take chances on their people. But they don't always maximize their role in a movement as much as they could. We must find them, map their relationships, and connect them within the broader network. The person who finds these champions is the linchpin to the extreme collaboration process — the catalyst.

3. Catalysts

These people are connectors. They run the network seams, brokering knowledge and connecting people.[12] Catalysts are the architects and stewards of stability tribes. For collaborative groups to form across organizational seams, it takes change agents who can stretch comfort zones and bring diverse groups together around a common problem. This is the catalyst.

Just as catalysts bond certain metals together in the world of chemistry, they are the connective tissue within the collaboration body. Brafman and Beckstrom define a catalyst as follows:

1. Catalysts develop ideas or initiatives.

2. Catalysts share these initiatives and ideas with others.

3. Catalysts lead by example.

4. When the time is right, catalysts step aside and let the movement take its course.[13]

Every organization has a catalyst. T.E. Lawrence was a catalyst. Hulsman makes this crystal clear: "Each of his masters, the Arabs and the British, tended to look at the revolt from his own specific perspective. More than anything else, Lawrence was the pivot point of the rebellion, the fulcrum that linked two very different peoples to a common cause."[14]

Catalysts find and amplify the voices of relevant experts that would otherwise not be heard. There are so many people out there who can contribute to solving wicked problems, but often they are overshadowed by the loudest person in the room. Or we simply don't find them because we don't know where to look. Catalysts do.

Catalysts are everywhere. Every organization has them. But you have to value them in order to find them. Are the catalysts in your organization visible to you? If not, they should be.

A note for senior leaders: Catalysts are assets to be identified and groomed. Champions should identify them, hone their skills and empower them. Learn from generals like Petraeus, Reeder, and Miller. Turn catalysts loose into socially complex networks to bring disparate worlds together for optimal results. Develop systems to identify and socially map catalysts across different organizations the same way we map target populations in counterinsurgency campaigns.

Now that we have our key players, we need to step into our unifying ideology.

4. Common belief system

Have you ever dreaded working with a rival organization, only to find it to be a pleasant experience because the person you worked with was awesome? They had the vision to think beyond their organizational charter and worked with you to achieve a bigger picture that made sense for both organizations. That person was a catalyst. You shared a common belief system that transcended the parochial culture of the organizations you both worked in.

True believers must be mobilized to change the game. These true believers rally around an existing stability ideology discovered through the 'hard knocks' of practical action.

For the stability problems we have identified, there is already an existing ideology out there. In fact, there are hundreds, if not thousands, of stability practitioners in all disciplines who subscribe to it. I have met with, fought alongside with, and supported more of them than I could name in this work. They are out there. Are you one of them?

The final ingredients to this collaborative process are the networks that each member comes from and draws from to bring his unique relevance to the tribe.

5. Pre-existing networks

Think of networks as the universe, and a stability tribe as a constellation within that universe. Networks provide stability tribes with "empowered membership, and typically have a higher tolerance for innovation."[15] In fact, networks have always been key to lasting change movements such as AA and the Quakers. Brafman and Beckstrom refer to them as "pre-existing networks."[16] The Internet and social media make these networks much more prevalent today.

Our stability tribe is fed by the networks of other tribe members. Many of these networks only talk to their own kind. When Major Ed asked me to lead the creation of Academic Week, it wasn't because he was lazy. We needed resource support from the large SOCOM headquarters for this event to work. Ed knew that as a member of SOCOM, I could go into that network and navigate waters he could not as an outsider.

This is where catalysts and champions make more strategic contributions. Coming from disparate networks, they connect and build tribes that leverage a common belief system around a shared problem. Catalysts and champions can then reach back into their unique pre-existing networks and build a stability tribe that works on the problem.

How collaboration empowers bottom-up

Extreme collaboration strategically empowers going local. Without it, VSO would have remained a tactical program that never developed. Instead, collaboration helped many local advisors overcome significant social issues and intimidation problems that were causing bottlenecks in potential stability gains. Collaboration tribes that stretched all the way to the University of California, Davis were built around local problems like agriculture to help communities solve their own problems. Isolation was shattered, and strategic outcomes, like increased food security, emerged across hundreds of Afghan villages.

This Game Changer, however, does more than create a "swarm" effect on wicked local problems. Collaboration is the reason VSO became a strategic program in Afghanistan.

Collaborate to change the game

I am passionate about all the Game Changers, but I am particularly passionate about collaboration. This is partly because I've learned to collaborate as a catalyst to achieve strategic results that I never thought possible. Some of these have involved the growth of VSO and the implementation of Academic Week. But I've also used it to build a multimillion-dollar real estate portfolio at home while deployed all over the Middle East, and to help raise millions of dollars for our military veterans. This type of extreme collaboration produces amazing results — everywhere.

But the other reason I am so passionate about this Game Changer is because almost no one does it. The potential of collaboration as a stability tool is beyond measure, yet we ignore it while violent extremists run circles around us. I am tired of watching amazingly talented leaders and practitioners bash their head against the impervious walls of organizational stovepipes as they try to solve stability problems they know are bigger than them or their organizations.

This has to change.

Regardless of the power of collaboration, some people will push back from this approach. Collaboration requires leaders to display 360 degrees of trust, which is hard for many to do. It's not just a communication issue.[17] It's a control issue. I'm talking budgetary 'rice bowls' here. The current process is rigid and some leaders cast a jaundiced eye at anything that is flat and flexible.

Other mid-level managers and staff members worry about collaboration replacing traditional authority. "They embrace the status quo and drown out any tribe member who dares to question authority and the accepted order," explains Godin.[18]

They shouldn't, because collaboration doesn't bypass leaders — it involves them more. "Folks who want to make change happen are surrounded by folks who don't get it. Some are scared or uninterested; others are pessimistic and full of their own self-importance. Those mindsets bog everyone down," caution William Bratton and Zachary Tumin.[19]

The relevant leaders today are the ones who can see through this self-defeating clutter to deftly navigate between policy, strategy, and tactics while artfully building stability tribes to solve hard problems. Catalysts who are comfortable enough in their own skin to not care about personal credit, and who reach across organizational gaps and seams to connect to other catalysts, will be at the heart of this effort.

Stability has life-and-death stakes. Traditionalists who worry about organizational legacy or losing control will become the losers as the game changes. Those not embracing collaboration will be left in the dust. It will be violent extremists who smile back at them through their rearview mirror as they drive toward global relevance, while the unchanged leaders sit blissfully unaware, sharpening their organizational knives for unilateral opportunities that will never come.

Miles to go

Today's military planning guidance talks glowingly about collaboration across seams and disciplines. USSOCOM, for example, promotes the "global SOF network." SOCOM describes this network of various actors as a "network built on trust."[20] This is very effective guidance, but as a community trying to achieve this guidance, we still have a long way to go.

To make this move from an industrial-age system to a relevant network environment that expands the pie by building on each other's strengths, all relevant stability agencies and organizations need to step up and collaborate. Not just the U.S. military.

Even with unprecedented collaboration and success, VSO was terminated well before its intended time. What derailed this strategic program and the overall Afghan campaign? *The absence of narrative.* We will talk about that in the next chapter.

Chapter Highlights

- *Collaboration in 21st-century stability operations is new and strategic.*

- *Stability knowledge gaps, isolation in a vast network, and an outdated problem-solving process plague all future efforts to defeat violent extremism.*

- *Collaboration reduces "transaction costs" in blood and treasure for solving stability problems.*

- *The stability collaboration framework consists of tribes, networks, a common belief system, champions, and catalysts.*

- *No matter how advanced we think we are, we are still more status society than contract society, which can adversely affect how we work together.*

- *To build tribes in contract society, we should go 'old school' and let our knowledge of status society inform and enhance our connections within contract society.*

- *Collaboration was the "secret sauce" to VSO and ALP becoming strategic.*

- *Collaboration can be replicated in other tough, bottom-up problem sets.*

Chapter 10

Lead with Story

"Those who tell stories, rule the world." — *Plato*

Arghandab District, 2010

The night started off like many other nights in rural Afghanistan: The sounds of a festive wedding were drifting lazily on the night air. Attendees were mostly Alikozai tribesmen and their families from the surrounding area. Many of them were local defenders of the Village Stability Program in Arghandab District. Men, women and children were mingling, feasting, and enjoying the celebration.

But not all of the attendees were there to celebrate. A young teenager from Pakistan was moving silently, and with purpose, around the cooking area. This would be his last night on earth, and he knew it. Posing as a servant, the only thing he would be serving tonight was death.

Suicide bombers are a high-value commodity within extremist networks. It takes time to persuade someone to kill himself, to train him, and to move him into the target area while avoiding detection. Extremist leaders know that targets need to be strategic and symbolic in order to justify the expenditure of this strategic commodity.

Tonight's target was a village — a village that had stood against the Taliban. This the Taliban feared so much that they deployed a suicide bomber against an entire village of civilians.

The Pakistani teen was carrying a large tray of rice. Beneath the tray was an improvised explosive device, courtesy of bomb makers in Quetta, Pakistan. As he neared the wedding party attendees, he detonated the device.

Many locals were simply vaporized, with others gravely wounded. Body parts hung from the trees. It was utter chaos.

All told, this heinous attack killed 40 Afghan civilians and gravely wounded 87 more.

Blowing yourself up doesn't come naturally. It isn't easy. Many would-be bombers get cold feet. Some have to be coerced at gunpoint. Others have had their hands tied to steering wheels of cars packed with explosives.

Despite their trepidations, many go through with it. They kill themselves in the name of their religion — for their families, for their honor.

So why does someone take his own life and the lives of others, especially, like in this case, where the victims are your own people and where suicide is reviled in tribal society?

They've been told a really good story.

The absence of story

This last Game Changer might come as a surprise. Storytelling? This is the 21st century, not Ancient Greece. Is storytelling really that important in this hyper-connected, fast-paced world?

You bet your Rudyard Kipling ass it is.

Just look at the influence of ISIS versus the U.S. in the Islamic world today. Whose story has framing and explanatory power right now? Theirs, or ours? Whose story is winning new recruits from all over the world? Violent extremists are running circles around us on YouTube and Facebook as we fumble for symbols and narratives to explain our policies, actions, and operations to ourselves, let alone the Muslim world.

We are a nation with tremendous storytelling at home — the biggest movie and book industry in the world. Yet we project almost no storytellers abroad. Strategic messaging, as we call it, has become so specialized and compartmentalized that anyone who brings it into the public forum becomes a lightning rod to professionals who deal in information for a living. Story has become so complex that most of us just omit it altogether from our stability activities.

Unless we are going to pursue total war against violent extremists, this avoidance of narrative must stop. Storytelling is a gaping hole in our capacity to defeat violent extremism.

"We have not yet learned to understand narrative and story as primary tools in the bio-technology of human cooperation," says narrative expert Doyle Quiggle, who lived and worked among many Afghan security forces as a teacher and advisor in east Afghanistan. Doyle was so adamant about understanding the Afghan narrative that he shared a tent with the Afghan security forces, interpreters, and camp workers for a year. "Yet the myth entrepreneurs of our enemies do understand story as a strategic tool for mobilizing fighters to their cause from around the globe," he concludes.[1]

It's as simple as this: It doesn't matter how many guns, bombs or soldiers we have. If we don't have a narrative that resonates with people, if we can't tell a story that people believe, we will not defeat violent extremists.

Instead, ISIS and groups like them will narrate the history of the 21st century.

Definitions

Because there are differing perspectives within the information community on the definition of story and narrative, let us start with a definition that comes from the Center for Strategic Communication,[2] with some modifications:

Story is a particular sequence of related past events recounted for ideological purposes. Story is where the rubber meets the road in persuasion and influence. Story is a welcome life raft of meaning and memory in a churning sea of data, facts, and sound bites. Stories are also "social proof" and carry an emotional component that moves us to action.

Social proof is an important aspect of group influence. You're new in town, and hungry. There are two restaurants. One is packed and the other is empty. Which one do you choose? Most people would choose the more crowded restaurant that shows social proof of being a good place to eat.

A *narrative* is a *coherent system of interrelated and sequentially organized stories.* These stories combine to form common desire and serve to resolve a conflict by establishing expectations. This narrative is communicated locally through effective storytelling.[3]

The *master narrative* is a grand story that has evolved throughout history through repetition and reverence. This narrative is born from conflict. It touches emotional chords, which create desire among followers, with a promise of some kind of satisfaction at the end of the struggle.

In the case of violent extremists, master narrative, narrative, and story are embedded deeply in religious culture and clan history. But it's not just violent extremists; this is also true from the Scots-Irish clans of Appalachia across the world to North Africa, where race, honor, and Bedouin lifestyles still reign.

So how was the Nagahan suicide bomber influenced by story?

"It is the nature of human beings to interpret the world around them through stories," write Halverson, Goodall, and Corman.[4] The teenage suicide bomber described above was likely told a compelling story in his Pakistani madrassa about how Afghan Local Police had emerged in this village. He was probably told other stories about how the bearded Special Forces soldiers living in the village were forcing locals to join this movement, or how these locals were actually sympathizers with the American infidels.

All of these *stories* supported the *narrative* that American occupation in rural Afghanistan is replacing the traditional codes and values of village elders. This *narrative* fed into *the master narrative* that this young man had heard his entire life: Tribal Islam is under attack by the West and it is the duty of every Muslim to defend it.

All of these elements of narrative and story were eloquently woven together to convince this young man that killing innocent women and children at a wedding actually served a higher purpose. His life was now fueled with meaning. This story recipe for suicide attacks mobilizes actions at all levels.

The power of story

The roaring engine of story has always driven big movements in history. Why?

Stories drive emotion, and emotion drives action.

Narratives and the stories that support them also win wars. Remember Thermopylae and the handful of Spartans who held that narrow pass at the cost of their own lives? Woven into a compelling narrative and retold thousands of times over in individual stories, it mobilized an entire nation to defend against Persia.

Story is the reason many Americans swell with pride after watching the opening scene of George C. Scott as the legendary General Patton in *Patton* (1970). It's why athletes rush the field to rally to a win after a rousing halftime speech from their coach. Stories persuade us to reach into our pockets at Christmastime to help the less fortunate. Hell, even

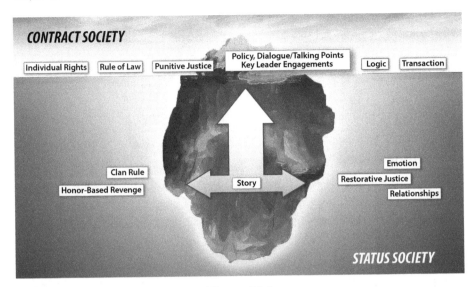

Figure 10-1.
The Power of Story in Both Societies
Because story is so biologically powerful in leveraging critical action through emotion, it is relevant in both status and contract society.Story is one of the best tools to use in honor-based clan societies. But story is also very powerful in contract society, where we still exhibit clan behavior but don't realize it. Story can positively influence a range of transactional components, ranging from PowerPoint decision briefs to million-dollar corporate deals.

New Coke had a story line. (I didn't say all stories worked. I simply said all big movements were tied to story. But I bet you at least tried New Coke, didn't you?)

"No matter how wonderful and fulfilling your body of work is, if you want people to believe in it, act on it, be moved by it, or buy it," says Pamela Slim in her book *Body of Work*, "you must shape it into a cohesive narrative and tell powerful stories."[5]

Think about your first job interview. Sitting across from you was an employer asking you why she should consider you for the job. How did you convince her to hire you above all the other dorks sitting in the waiting room?

Now think about the toughest proposal you ever had to pitch at work. It meant convincing skeptics who were not in favor of change. Resistance was heavy on all sides. How did you handle it?

It's early in the morning on a crisp, fall day. You're standing at a bus stop with your child on her first day of school. It's not clear who has the bigger lump in their throat, you or the little one who's death-clinging to your leg. How do you convince her to take that terrifying first step onto the bus?

Story is the answer to all of the questions above.

Why stories matter

Stories are deeply embedded in our DNA. They're a central part of any status society, but they affect us deeply in contract society as well. From the first grunts, hand waving, and cave paintings to YouTube on our smart-phones, story still resonates deeply within us.

Traditionally, story was not just about entertainment, it was about passing on crucial cultural knowledge or driving people to specific action.

Even in total-war scenarios like WWII, Hollywood director Frank Capra crafted stories entitled *Why We Fight* to mobilize large numbers of Americans to defeat Nazi Germany. Every newsreel, every poster was a story that was a larger part of the WWII narrative.[6]

Stories work because they reach us emotionally, and emotion is what drives people to perform meaningful actions, not just reason. "We have an intuitive, emotional side, as well as a deliberate, rational side to our character," say storytelling experts from thestorytellers.com. "Too often in business, we only try and connect with people on a rational level, but this isn't enough to actually change how people behave. People may understand what you want them to do but if they aren't emotionally engaged they just won't do it!"[7]

Even in this fast-paced, transactional world, stories are critical ele-ments of how we make decisions. Whether it's deciding to buy a new TV for your home, which college to attend, or who to vote for, the story and the storyteller will play a major role in your decision.

In this highly connected world of YouTube and Facebook, we are disconnected without story. "When facts become so widely available and instantly accessible, each one becomes less valuable. What begins to matter more is the ability to place these facts in context, and to deliver them with emotional impact," says author Daniel Pink in his book *A Whole New Mind*.[8]

Well-done stories tug at our deepest biological levels. The neuro-economist Paul Zak has done in-depth research that reveals people experience strong biological reactions during well-told stories. For instance, when conflict and struggle are part of a story, our brain emits cortisol to promote focus. During the climax portion of stories, our brain emits oxytocin, which promotes connection and empathy, and when the resolution of story is revealed — you know, the happy ending — the brain's limbic system releases a healthy batch of dopamine to promote a feeling of optimism.[9] These biological responses run deep, create powerful human connections, and transcend every culture and society.

Violent extremists know this and apply it in every aspect of their information campaign. "Just as ISIS has used captured American artillery against its enemies in Iraq, so it is using the West's media tools and techniques against it," warns *Guardian* reporter Steve Rose. "ISIS has proved fluent in YouTube, Twitter, Instagram, Tumblr, Internet memes (see: #catsofjihad) and other social media."[10]

Just as story motivates suicide bombers to do their worst, however, story can also move each of us to do our best. Zak's research even indicated that when people were asked to donate to total strangers, those who heard stories that elicited emissions of oxytocin were more likely to donate more money to total strangers than those who were not told a story, but instead given a briefing on the same nonprofit issue.[11] Everything that means something to us is tied through story, including the modern wars we wage.

The unfortunate irony is that as impactful as storytelling is to us at home, we don't do a very good job of telling stories abroad.

A war of narratives

Dr. Tom Johnson describes the Afghan campaign as a "war of narratives."[12] This is also true of our broader global fight against violent extremists. If this is true, then we are losing this war. Story and master narrative are especially pronounced in the Islamic world. Their narratives and stories are resonating with key audiences in ways that we aren't even challenging.

Extremist leadership crafts a master narrative deeply rooted in Islam, regional history, and tribal culture. Per Halverson, Goodall, and Corman, "The reinstatement of the Caliphate, the implementation of shari'ah law, or the expulsion of the 'Crusaders' from their lands forms a powerful source of narrative satisfaction, despite the fact that many of those hoped-for-events have not occurred."[13] Extremist narratives also take on a tribal flair, which invokes actions of honor and revenge.

These narratives tap into the emotional components of a downtrodden Muslim world (*Ummah*) by portraying a historically victimized group of faithful followers that is preordained for greatness, but held back by enemies of Islam (that's us). This master narrative directs that it is the duty of every Muslim to strike these enemies wherever they are.

Islamist leaders are competing with us for the support of their religious base, potential fighters, donors, nonbeliever populations, and even our own people in the U.S. In fact, violent extremist groups like ISIS, al Qa'ida, and the Taliban are very crafty at developing key audience segments for influence. They then develop objectives, stories, mediums, and tellers appropriate for each audience. And we make it very easy for them.

Their focused storytelling to segmented groups produces strategic outcomes. Millions offer up prayers. Others donate large sums of money. Many volunteer to fight the infidels in support of jihad. Some even offer their lives unconditionally by agreeing to commit suicide attacks.

At home, we observe these acts by committed ideologues and can't agree how to respond. We wonder how we should respond. Our dysfunctional internal narrative gap and our disinterest in story abroad make us unwitting participants in a strategic bait-and-switch to draw us in even deeper. Because we don't understand their reality, we try to force our Western story into their Islamic status society context, which comes across as not credible and even threatening.

Violent extremists, by contrast, create a narrative of imminent victory and inclusive membership in a better society.[14] As they push this narrative down from the top, they also pull from the bottom — selectively comparing their actions to ours every step of the way, in thousands of individual stories. These stories serve as social proof of their master narrative that 'Islam is under attack from the West,' a message constantly reinforced through video, blogs, and good old-fashioned oral storytelling.

Some stories include video footage of extremist suicide attacks or gun battles with Western forces or government security forces. These digital stories also include American servicemen urinating on the corpses of dead Taliban fighters, the burning of Korans, and the bodies of women and children killed in drone strikes and air raids. Whether these stories are real or fabricated, it doesn't matter — our story isn't even there.

Violent extremists also embed with locals by incorporating local grievances into their master narratives. For example, al Qa'ida in the

Islamic Maghreb (North Africa) won the Tuareg tribes over to their cause by addressing their local grievances with the government of Mali, only to lose them later by targeting their tribal practices of Sufi mysticism as non-Islamic. Narrative gaps exist on both sides. This is an opportunity for us.

The Tuareg example shows that violent extremists are far from perfect in narrative and storytelling. Although they are winning the war of narrative, they often contradict themselves and their message at every turn. They prey on local populations, terrorize minorities, and violate the Koran and its teachings. We just don't amplify it when they do. However, one veteran Mauritanian filmmaker did just that with his recent release, *Timbuktu.*

In this movie, Abderrahmane Sissako demonstrates the oppression and hypocrisy of Islamist violent extremists operating in Mali's capital. He calls these extremists out on their double standards on everything from soccer to smoking, and how they treat women. "By rendering his enemy ridiculous, he also renders him impotent," writes John Anderson of Sissako in a *New York Times* interview.[15]

The U.S. could certainly take a lesson or two from this approach of shining the light of truth on the local behavior of these extremists, just like Frank Capra did against Hitler during WWII.

Our problems with story run deep

Before we can address ways to change the game through story, we need to look deeply at our current challenges. There are three major issues we have in relation to narrative and storytelling, as they pertain to defeating violent extremism. First, we lack a credible master narrative to compete with the narratives crafted by violent extremists. Second, we are ill prepared to tell stories at a local level. And third, we don't leverage local stories as social proof of our master narrative. These gaps were very pronounced in Iraq and Afghanistan, but they are popping up in new 'hot spots' all over the globe, including the U.S. and Western Europe. They will cause us to lose if we don't change. Let's look closer.

The U.S. lacks credible narratives against violent extremists

> *"You Americans have merely been talking to yourselves."*[16]

> — Afghan National Army soldier

"Even with the best of intentions to bring stability and betterment to Afghan society, the U.S. falls into the role of the 'colonizing invader' and we don't even realize it," says Doyle Quiggle. "The honor-shame dynamic is ruthlessly exploited by the Taliban master narrative."[17]

Remember early in the Global War on Terror when our national leaders talked about bringing democracy to the Middle East and Afghanistan? This was a terrible Western master narrative that actually gave fuel to the extremist flame. It failed to consider Islamic culture and history. It also completely ignored clan society's cultural values of group needs over individual needs.

Who needs story when you have drones?

"This war can be won with drones" is another misplaced narrative to our own people, which feeds the extremist narrative. Some lethal targeting is necessary to remove irreconcilable extremists from the battlefield. Done in isolation with no local presence, however, it dramatically degrades our effectiveness.[18]

"Drone attacks make it worse. Much like the dark memories of the Soviet Hind helicopters that strafed rural Afghan villages, drones have become the feared harbinger of death and destruction from the West," writes Eliza Grizwold in her in-depth study, conducted across Afghanistan.

The U.S. drone is building its place in Afghan poetry, known as Landays, by replacing the Soviet attack helicopter as the faceless manifestation of evil in tribal society. "Even for those locals who hate the Taliban, the fear of drones has helped to drive support for the militants, as they're seen as the only ones brave enough to fight the occupation of land and now the sky," concludes Grizwold.[19]

SOF raids in Africa and limited air strikes in Syria have similar effects in promoting the extremist master narrative. This is not my opposition to surgical strikes; we need them. This is opposition to surgical strikes that tie into no relevant local narrative.

We minimize narrative and story when the stakes are high

When it comes to stability activities, we have divorced ourselves from narrative and story. The people who are responsible for designing our narrative and communicating our stories are often not the people who will conduct the actions. Story is an afterthought. Our planning and

critical thinking on story development and delivery are very dispropor-
tionate from our lethal actions.

Oh sure, we consider it. "What story are we putting out to the locals?"
is a question that many military commanders ask their staff. Unfortunately, it's usually as the bombs are hurling toward preselected targets
or as operators are boarding aircraft for a midnight strike.

In today's military and government stability activities, we typically
export the narrative responsibility to our strategic communications, information operations, and psychological operations organizations. This
means that operators and practitioners won't have to deal with it so they
can focus on lethal targeting. It then becomes a compartmentalized
function. That means practitioners closest to the simmering grievances,
and most capable of connecting to the human solution, lose our input
on narrative and the ability to tell our story. This approach is ineffective.

If we really believe that we can't kill our way to victory in these stability interventions, then we should do a much better job of crafting powerful narratives and storytelling in order to influence key audiences. This
includes broadening the scope of storytellers to include those who must
ultimately conduct the local actions. You really do get what you pay for
in these situations.

So where does that leave us?

This capacity gap in narrative and storytelling has us losing the fight
against violent extremists on every level. The narrative problem in
Afghanistan has degraded so badly that counterinsurgency expert
Anthony Cordesman has said the U.S. in Afghanistan should change its
focus from achieving its strategic goals to "minimizing strategic failure."
Unbelievable.

While I might concede the need to do some damage control in Afghanistan and Iraq, I find it very depressing that this is the best practice we're
carrying into new challenges, like Syria. Even the racial tensions in Ferguson, Missouri and the growing anti-establishment movement against
local police in the U.S. show evidence of this defeatist, risk-mitigation
approach to storytelling.

The impact of losing the narrative war abroad or at home is unacceptable. History casts a dark shadow over those that do. It could mean
mass mobilization of Islamist extremists upon the U.S. and its allies in
unprecedented ways. It is not beyond the pale to think that an Islamist
narrative that prevails as legitimate could result in sustained attacks

against everyday Americans, a catastrophic attack within our borders, or even a growth of Sharia-based clan society inside the U.S.

As we tuck our own children into bed at night as the hero in their world, we should know that we are also the 'boogey man' in the late-night dreams of millions of other children throughout the Islamic world. This narrative, promoted by violent extremists, gives them local legitimacy by projecting us as the 'evil invader.' Meanwhile, they portray themselves as protectors and leaders of their people. They don't do this from a distance, like we do. They do this locally, from within the community.

These deeply embedded safe havens become the workshops of future terror attacks, international crime, and other strategic threats to the U.S. and its allies. Do you see how story actually gives extremists this local presence, social proof, and strategic advantage over us?

What can be done?

We don't have to accept the current trajectory of narrative defeat. The U.S. has an amazing storytelling capacity that matches its capacity for meaningful action. We have proven throughout our history that we are capable of crafting a narrative that speaks to a higher purpose. This mobilizes people and groups to take meaningful action in spite of arduous conditions, and to achieve the desired outcome of this master narrative.

These stories should be told locally, and bottom-up through VSO and community engagement.

There are five practical steps we can implement to strategically enhance narrative and story:

1. Craft narratives that stick and tell them well.

Locals standing up for their way of life is a very powerful narrative in almost any honor-based clan society. The rapid spread of VSO throughout Day Kundi and Oruzgan provinces shows just how powerful it can be. Local autonomy is a potential master narrative to bridge two very different cultures of East and West. It resonates with the Islamic audience, especially in informal clan areas beyond the reach of the government. This is because it empowers locals to stand on their own — which rings true as historically appropriate.

Local autonomy also resonates with the U.S. because it involves indigenous populations, not large formations of U.S troops, standing up on their own. This means less commitment of U.S. blood and treasure. The narrative can also show how it makes our country safer. Local resistance to violent extremism is much less invasive to clan society. Therefore, it is less likely to invoke clan revenge in the form of terror attacks against our homeland.

This narrative can be further expanded to include fragile governments that lack trust with their clan societies. It would look something like this: "Clan societies are standing up for themselves, supported by their government..." Some might be thinking, there is no way the partner government will ever agree to this.

I get it. It is a tough sell. But it is a sell we can make. This is no tougher than trying to persuade unruly clans to support a Western-style government they don't understand or trust. In fact, it's easier. Working with partner nations, like the Shia-based Iraqi government, we can bring to bear our instruments of power, such as foreign aid and military support, to persuade these governments to be more inclusive of narratives that favorably mobilize Sunni tribes and other minority ethnic groups.

We should emphasize with our partner nations that if they want the capacity for long-term stability, they also need to play ball with internal local realities. Our diplomatic efforts should provide narrative top-cover that encourages foreign governments to connect with their marginalized clan societies. By crafting their role as responsibly supporting informal civil society, host governments can make lasting connections, and over time, move toward cohesion as a state. That is narrative in action.

Many powerful narratives already exist, if we open our eyes to the possibilities, even if they don't fit our biased Western lens. Historical clan autonomy and clan distrust of outsiders are two examples where narratives can be leveraged. Our ignorance of existing narratives, such as these, is just another reason why we need to change the game.

This is a paradigm change for our intelligence community as well. They have to get well beyond the threat networks and into the world of narrative. We should identify the narratives that are already out there resonating with key audience groups, and why. This is a very important collection requirement that is not happening. Not enough leaders are calling for narrative perspective as an information requirement; when they do, the intelligence community will respond to this demand.

We should also highlight the contradictions of the violent extremists in violation of their religion and their professed ideology. Violent extremists prey on local villagers — they beat them, they behead them, they take from them, they marginalize the roles of resilient leaders, and commit many other violations, all while claiming globally to stand for those villagers. This is often the reason that many groups, like some Sunni tribes, resist ISIS. We should show the extremists honestly as the thugs they really are.

Extremist groups and malign actors often behave badly; we're just too biased or politically correct to embrace how the game is played and call them out on it. Our focus on dismantling terror networks and top-down counterinsurgency programs like 'government in a box' is what blinds us. We need to take the blinders off and amplify these extremist narrative contradictions locally and internationally until — as with the FARC in Colombia — they are no longer viewed as ideologues, but irrelevant thugs who prey on the people. This proven approach can be replicated as part of larger narrative anywhere in the world, and it's high time we did so.

Lead with good stories and follow them with action

Telling stories locally is essential 'Lawrencian' stability tradecraft. Storytelling in everyday, local conversations while conducting VSO can be very powerful; it can change ideology. These stories serve as social validation for narratives and master narratives. Telling the story of Tamazan villagers revolting against extremist control did two things. First, it amplified the narrative of extremists preying on locals. Second, it was social proof of the Afghan narrative of clans and villages standing up for themselves. This resonated at strategic levels in the U.S. and across Afghanistan and led to significant expansion of stability highlighted in Chapter 5.

Before we leave the topic of how we should tell our stories, I want to cover one more thing. The brushfire expansion of VSO from Tamazan Village deep into Oruzgan Province worked for two major reasons, and they both revolved around a combination of story and action.

The first was that Green Berets and other Special Operators told village elders that they would help their community reestablish its traditional autonomy. These operators emphasized that the village, not outsiders, should determine security and stability. This narrative connected deeply with the honor-based traditions and austerity of these rural communities.

Second, advisors also told local leaders they would stay with them and fight when things got bad. And when things got bad, that's exactly what these operators did. And things usually got bad quickly. Once word spread in the form of oral story that locals were reclaiming their communities with the help of special operators, it provided social proof of our commitment to would-be resistance movements in other communities.

This is powerful stuff in honor society. People act on how you move them emotionally through your story and your deeds. Story without action is meaningless. This is why narratives at strategic and policy levels must be informed with local and tactical actions on the ground. Special operators were risking life and limb to live among rural Afghans, all while U.S. policy called for withdrawal of forces and President Karzai called for special operators to come out of the villages. This is a major reason why there is such a trust deficit among local populations and the U.S.–supported governments.

Some refer to this as a 'say-do' gap. Where I come from, we simply call it bullshit. Designing clever terms for describing how we bullshit people is exactly what gives us these credibility problems. Do you know when someone is bullshitting you? I sure do. In clan society, they can smell it a mile away. People have to believe your story and in your narrative before they will act. Perhaps if we stop making narrative and story such a specialized cerebral, elitist skill, we won't have this issue.

2. Make narrative design and storytelling a team sport.

We should stop outsourcing and overspecializing story. We have made story too hard. It has become extremely confusing to influence people or to gain permission to do so. We have divested ourselves of this requirement and outsourced it to a handful of organizations that have built firewalls around their own domain.

I recall numerous times in Afghanistan when we waited over 48 hours to disseminate local facts about Taliban bombings that killed innocent local Afghans. By the time we gained permission from senior headquarters, the Taliban had long since blamed it on us and garnered local support.

Story is timeless and runs deep within each of us. When working in at-risk areas, however, we dilute it with our Western contract society biases and tech-speak. This simply widens the trust gap between community and government that is already there. We have moved away from what is instinctive and compelling through storytelling to what must be learned through a PhD and is as dry as the Sahara sand. In doing so, we have lost the ability to move and influence people at emotional levels to achieve a higher purpose.

I am not crashing down on those who influence and persuade for a living. These folks do great work. I am coming down on the rest of us who have outsourced and devalued the element of story to them alone. Our narrative, and how we tell it, is a team sport.

3. Build a narrative tribe.

Here is another example where the Game Changers work best when used together. To craft a narrative and tell stories skeptical audiences will believe, we need narratives and stories that cross cultural and organizational boundaries. We can't do that "talking to ourselves," as our Afghan Army friend cautioned us. We need to build a very diverse 'narrative tribe' using the extreme collaboration techniques from the previous chapter. This tribe should include relevant interagency and private sector parties, players from the partner government, as well as status society community members.

How do we get State Department representatives, NGOs, Green Berets, moderate Islamic leaders, and village elders around the same table to establish a master narrative? It wouldn't hurt to go back and reread Chapter 8, "Meet Them Where They Are." This is a big challenge. We can't allow parochialism to stop us from crafting a master narrative.

We have great storytellers among us. When building our 'narrative tribe,' we should bring in narrative, storytelling, and marketing expertise from outside the government as well. The U.S. has Madison Avenue, Hollywood, academia, and others who could provide significant contributions to this tribe. Why aren't they part of our solution? Why aren't we asking for their help? With all the hyped-up talk about private-public partnership, wouldn't this Madison Avenue–Hollywood–U.S. government tribe be a great opportunity for that?

And let's not forget including members who can help us gain local clarity on pre-existing master narratives. There are plenty of resilient groups and credible voices standing up to extremism under narratives that already resonate with local communities. We must include in our 'narrative tribe' those who can collect this information and share it for increased use.

The narrative tribe not only helps us craft realistic narratives, it also helps us find the best strategic and local storytellers. The strategic storytellers should be our champions. These senior leaders and public figures should be able to draft and deliver a powerful narrative that local storytellers can feed into.

An example of these strategic storytellers might be the Iraqi and U.S. presidents proclaiming an enduring commitment to help marginalized Sunnis stand up for themselves against the criminal behavior of al Qa'ida and ISIS. These narratives can set conditions for powerful results informed by local stories.

These local storytellers can come from a vast audience that includes tribal leaders, farmers, and religious leaders. Our 'narrative tribes' can play a big role in finding and leveraging them. There are numerous potential local stories, ranging from Iraqi Special Forces helping Sunni communities defend against violent extremists to ISIS committing atrocities against locals. These stories are social proof in support of these narratives.

Our own embedded advisors, such as Marine special operators and Green Berets, are also critical to this group of local storytellers. They must be trained and positioned to live and work among the people conducting the bottom-up actions that carry their own powerful story from ridgeline to ridgeline. This type of local storytelling requires a deep 'Lawrencian' skill set we currently don't have.

4. Build a capacity for narrative competence and storytelling.

What do T.E. Lawrence, Mullah Mike, and Salinas Police Chief Kelly McMillan all have in common? Well, in addition to achieving strategic results by going local, they were all excellent storytellers. In other words, they had narrative competence. I define narrative competence as *the dynamic ability to form deep human connections and influence strategic outcomes through the integrated employment of storytelling, active listening, and highly attuned inter-personal connection skills*.

In my experience, narrative competence is a severely - neglected skillset for going local. Most politicians, policy makers, senior military leaders, and tactical leaders lack this skill. Yet done well, it can produce strategic results from the policy levels of an embassy all the way down to an isolated desert village. The U.S. government, law enforcement, and even corporate America should expand training in narrative competence to leaders at all levels. It is essential for closing gaps and connecting top to bottom.

5. Create stories by matching activities on the ground with the narrative objectives.

Social proof is critical to advancing a master narrative that promotes relative stability and makes violent extremists irrelevant. Every day there are resilient community leaders who stand up to extremist intimidation, local government leaders who connect to rural communities, and violent extremists who overtly brutalize innocent civilians. Why aren't we maximizing these powerful stories?

These actions simply dissipate like the proverbial tree falling in the forest unless we capture and amplify them through story. While a peasant defending his home, in spite of a public threat of extremist retribution, might not seem like much, it is a powerful force of nature when told as a story that feeds a larger narrative. This is how our enemy does business and how we must change our game to defeat them.

It begins and ends with story

So far, our use of narrative and story has been a strategic failure. Crafting an ineffective master narrative after September 11th, 2001 resulted in our own people calling us home from Iraq and Afghanistan before the mission was complete. The extremists, meanwhile, have returned to their former safe havens, and are gaining strength. We are now facing even more ominous extremist threats, and with no guiding narrative as to the exact danger we face, or a call to action.

If key audiences, including our own people and our own leaders, don't believe our story, then we should consider doing nothing as our first option. Our blood and treasure are too precious to spend on campaigns that have no winds of story behind their sail. If we are going to continue to omit narrative and story from our actions, I also propose we consider a World War II–style approach of total attrition warfare against our enemies, including the undergoverned states in which they thrive. While this might sound extreme, the threat posed by violent extremists certainly justifies this type of action. Though much less desirable than the Game Changers proposed here, it is a more viable strategy than the actions taken over the last decade to project soft power in a hard shell, with no central narrative to guide us.

The horrific carnage sewn by the suicide bomber at the Nagahan Village wedding is a stark reminder of how influential narrative and story can be imposed upon those willing to harm us. By the same token, we also caught a glimpse of the positive brushfire effect that a narrative rooted in clan autonomy, and fueled by deeds of uprisings in local story, had in the expansion of VSO from Tamazan Village across West Oruzgan Province. The ideal solution is to tap into our vast, native potential for storytelling, get our narrative straight, and then tell it well.

Chapter Highlights

- *Stories consume every level of our life and, through their emotional connections, drive us to action.*

- *Master narratives are sequences of story rooted in history and culture, born from conflict, which mobilize people to strategic action.*

- *We are in a war of narratives with violent extremism — and we are losing.*

- *Story is a powerful tool that works universally in status and contract society.*

- *The influence of extremist ideology can be changed through compelling stories in everyday conversation — this is why going local with VSO and story go hand-in-hand.*

- *We need to create diverse narrative tribes to craft master narratives and choose the right storyteller.*

- *If our actions don't match our words, we are not credible and we will fail.*

PART III

Into Action

Chapter 11

Bypassing the Graveyard

Kabul, Afghanistan, Summer 2014

While writing this chapter, I had the opportunity to go back to Afghanistan. I went back to assess a few areas for the soon-departing Major General Miller related to VSO and collaboration.

I flew into Kabul on a worn-down civilian airliner with Safi Airlines. As I bounced around the air pockets of the bright blue sky above the mighty Afghan Hindu Kush, a profound sadness came over me.

This assessment would hold no surprises, because little has changed.

Our current policy in Afghanistan is failing. Our transition plan is putting our national security at unacceptable risk. Unless we make significant changes to our current approach, the U.S. will be another headstone in the Afghan graveyard of empires. We are leaving Afghanistan at a time when they desperately need us, and much earlier than needed for a capacity-building mission.

All of the blood and treasure we spent, and for what? The stated goals and strategy of extremist groups such as al Qa'ida and ISIS are unchanged. They fully intend to expand into other areas. If we leave them unchecked in Afghan rural safe havens, they will come for us with deadly unconventional tactics ranging from machetes to dump trucks to forest fires.

It doesn't have to be this way.

So while I was in Afghanistan for that last trip, I asked myself, "What if we decided to change things and get it right in Afghanistan? How would we use the Game Changers we learned late in the war to turn things around for a long-term win against violent extremists?"

Thirteen points to taking the bypass...

There is a better way to bypass the Afghan graveyard that allows us to learn from our best practices and thus overcome our past mistakes. In a world where policymakers and security experts profess only three inappropriate options — counterinsurgency; counterterrorism; or complete withdrawal — there is a better and more cost-effective, fourth option.

The following recommendations are directly informed by the four Game Changers previously covered. They are all nested within the context of a whole-of-nation government program called Foreign Internal Defense (FID).

FID is a long-term, small-footprint and whole-of-nation approach, led by the U.S. country team, which requires less U.S. blood and treasure. The proposal that follows includes U.S. and Afghan Special Operations Forces advising regular and irregular host nation forces to achieve relative stability in a country largely dominated by honor-based, status society.

This outline is specific to the ever-evolving violent extremist global threat model. Therefore, with some modifications of course, it is also applicable to many other 'hot spots' like Syria and Yemen.

1. Set an Afghan policy and strategy we can live with.

U.S. and NATO policy have never been effective or coherent in dealing with Afghanistan. After September 11th, we made a lot of emotional and uninformed choices. For example, we helped install many of the same armed warlords who had torn the country apart and had terrorized local populations in the 1990s.

We confused government for governance. We ignored the critical role that traditional governance plays in rural areas and relentlessly pushed a corrupt Afghan government onto a skeptical and traumatized Afghan civil society, opening ourselves up to a ready-made strategic Taliban narrative.

Don't leave your friends

Regardless of where the fickle winds of politics might blow, it is a bad idea to abandon your friends in politics, just as in personal life. This includes the rural villagers who stepped up and risked their lives for VSO in Afghanistan, the interpreters who fought and bled with us, and the brave Afghans who defied extremism in an attempt to rebuild an Afghan government. Perhaps our greatest loss from this transition is the trust and credibility we had built in so many rural communities on a local, personal level.

"We threw our local allies under the bus," said Dr. Ted Callahan, who worked closely with VSO leaders in Afghanistan. Ted is still in Afghanistan and has seen the impact of Special Operations Forces leaving the rural villages. "My old Afghan cell phone from my days with SOF rings off the hook from local Afghans who stood up as Afghan Local Police against extremists. It's heartbreaking to hear them plead for assistance after getting hammered by extremists all summer."[1]

In a society where trust is currency, our foreign policy is bankrupt.

Emerging hotspots like Syria and Libya indicate that U.S. strategic interventions at a local level are in our future. How do you make a case to a local villager to stand up against extremists in a place like Syria, when you just abandoned a guy in Afghanistan who was doing the same thing? People pay much more attention to the things we do and the promises we break than we think they do.

Deal sternly with Pakistan

It's time for us to toughen up on Pakistan. No matter how much we change the game in Afghanistan, relative stability will be impossible if Pakistan continues to provide sanctuary to violent extremists and foment instability inside Afghanistan's sovereign borders.

Pakistan is providing sanctuary to our enemies. They are actively working against Afghanistan and the coalition through proxy Taliban, Haqqani network members, and other insurgent groups, while simultaneously accepting billions of dollars in U.S. aid to supposedly help us fight terror. My grandfather used to say this type of duplicity meant someone "was pissing on your back while telling you it was raining."

We have very effective U.S. instruments of national power, which can be brought to bear in this situation — at a minimum, foreign aid — which to date, have been recklessly employed. We should at least stop foreign aid, impose sanctions, and possibly pursue even tougher military measures if Pakistan is going to campaign against Afghanistan and us.

2. Stop projecting Western biases and meet them where they are.

Afghanistan will likely never live up to our Western expectations. Who cares? That's not the point. We're looking for a country that can handle its own affairs and is inhospitable to violent extremists with global reach. We need to flush what we think we know about that country and really look at local reality. It starts by meeting them where they are and redefining relative stability to guide our actions.

3. Look at other models of success.

We should stop treating Afghanistan as the first insurgency we've ever dealt with in a budget-constrained, high-risk environment. We've actually got a history of doing these types of activities successfully in places like El Salvador, the Philippines, and Colombia, just to name a few.

In the winter of 1997, as a young Special Forces captain in 7th Special Forces Group, I conducted my first Special Forces deployment to another host nation fighting an insurgency, Colombia. Our mission was to work with the U.S. Embassy Country Team, DEA, and Colombian counternarcotic forces to stem the production and flow of cocaine into the U.S.

Seven months later I returned home convinced that Colombia and our efforts there were doomed to failure. The U.S. counternarcotics policy was a joke. The embassy interagency squabbling was paralyzing. Colombian President Andres Pastrana gave the FARC guerrillas a government-sanctioned safe haven the size of Switzerland, from which they projected unrest all over the country. The Colombian Army would not leave its bases. It was horrible.

I remember riding home on that airplane thinking Colombia was on its way to becoming a failed state and a foreign policy disaster.

Look at Colombia today. It is like a different country. In the last decade, Colombia has undergone a radical transformation, which has resulted in a robust economy, an invitation to participate in the Organization for Economic Cooperation and Development, and an enhanced capacity to project security assistance in our Western hemisphere. Yes, there are still problems. But there is much to learn from this effort for today's conflicts. For example, why not have our U.S. advisors bring Afghan civilian and military leaders to Colombia, to meet and observe with their political and military counterparts there to discuss best practices and lessons learned?

4. Get the long-term mission right.

Since Counterinsurgency (COIN) didn't succeed in Afghanistan, Counter-Terrorism (CT) is emerging as the primary mission. Many senior leaders like former Vice President Biden are huge proponents of this approach. CT in Afghanistan consists of drone strikes and Special Operations raids. Even our host nation capacity building is focused solely on direct action forces, an approach that has failed for over a decade.

These types of attacks on terror cells are not as clean as they appear on grainy screens in command centers. These attacks from the sky and night-home raids invoke "codes of honor and revenge, which will lead to escalating global violence," says Akbar Ahmed, author of *The Thistle and the Drone*.[2] Islamists mobilize entire clans to seek *badal* (revenge) against us.

SOF raids, advocated by President Trump, aren't much better. These types of attacks, usually at night, also have a profound negative effect on local communities, especially during home invasions. A captured extremist from a Special Operations raid on an Afghan compound might be a temporary benefit, but it is often considered a Pyrrhic victory, which will likely mobilize many other family and community members to pursue revenge against us for lost honor.

And let's not forget the "zero option," which appears to be an attractive option for the Trump administration's Afghan plan. Total disengagement from any at-risk area where violent extremists are establishing safe haven is a bad idea. Our complete disengagement from Afghanistan in the early 1980s, following the Soviet occupation and the subsequent nightmare scenario of civil war, Taliban rule, and the September 11th terror attacks, should give us a clue how bad the "zero option" is for post-2016 Afghanistan.

'Old-school' actions

"The model that American policymakers should look to for appropriate engagement of foreign governments in conflict zones is the FID [Foreign Internal Defense] and irregular warfare conducted by Special Operations forces."[3] This comment by Steve Thomas in his essay on "Rugged Diplomats" emphasizes the type of mission set needed for Afghanistan. I am amazed at how many government and military leaders have forgotten about, or simply ignore this historically effective foreign policy approach.

FID is a whole-of-nation, light-footprint, long-term approach to stability that has worked in a range of other countries. It is a proven way to stabilize contentious areas over the long haul. FID is well suited to deal with violent extremists who embed deep in informal status societies around the world, whether urban or rural.

We need counterterror actions, but they should not be our lead approach. They should be under the umbrella of a broader FID campaign that stabilizes rural areas, not targets them.

5. Get our story straight.

Once we straighten out our policy and mission set in Afghanistan, let's craft a compelling narrative that communicates this to critical audiences — and tell it well. This is Storytelling 101. And as we've learned, we suck at it! If we don't get this right, we'll never prevail.

In concert with the Afghan government and community leaders, let's develop a master narrative that resonates fearlessly from our national leaders in a way that demonstrates we are with Afghanistan and its people until they are ready to stand on their own.

Actions and deeds need to match our narratives. For instance, local villages overcame their fear of retribution and stood beside SOF in many VSO sites. They did this not because of words. They did this because the special operators who lived in their communities went to the rooftops and fought when danger came. They actually cared about daily village grievances. They backed up their word with local actions and deeds. This attitude is needed at every political level, not just villages.

Our enemies should see coalition and Afghan leaders jointly proclaiming a combined approach to stabilizing Afghanistan over the long term. This is potentially devastating to extremists salivating over future control in the next few months. Our persistent bilateral cooperation, informed by leaders in the right places, promotes determined growth of societal capacity from the inside out, which renders violent extremists irrelevant in the eyes of locals.

6. Leverage the network.

Extreme collaboration is critical. Afghanistan's social problems are so wickedly complex that no one entity can address them alone. Afghan civil society issues come from security, development, and governance — not just security. These grievances are fuel for the extremist fire. Helping Afghans overcome these broad challenges will require the integration of all U.S. instruments of power, instruments that usually don't play well together.

Consider again the USSOCOM Academic Week training sessions. These venues brought thousands of stability practitioners from disparate government civilian agencies, NGOs, Special Operations Forces, and conventional military units together. They familiarized attendees with complex stability problems like tribal dynamics, low-tech agriculture, development programs, and insider threats. Instructors came from the U.S. State Department, USAID, USDA, and even leaders from three Afghan ministries.

Ninety-five percent of operators rated Academic Week as being "extremely useful to pre-mission training." Pre-deployment connections were often cited as the greatest benefit of this training. These events are no longer funded by USSOCOM or supported during Afghan transition. They should be right-sized and re-implemented — not just in Afghanistan, but for other at-risk areas as well.

7. Put the U.S. Embassy in charge.

For a whole-of-nation approach to work properly, the U.S. Embassy — not a U.S. or NATO military headquarters — should be in charge. This is currently true in every other place where the U.S. intervenes, except Afghanistan.

A large military headquarters ran the campaign in Afghanistan for nearly 14 years. This structure marginalized diplomacy, development, and law enforcement. It also delayed the normal interagency activities necessary to achieve whole-of-nation solutions in working with a partner nation.

Granted, the security situation in Afghanistan is terrible, making it very tough for embassy officials. It will be painful at first. When you are the '800-pound DOD gorilla,' as our civilian counterparts often refer to us, it's tough to give up control. But let's face it, from Vietnam to Iraq, U.S. counterinsurgency campaigns are generally unsuccessful when the military is in charge. The sooner we wake up to this reality, the sooner we'll have viable stability in Afghanistan.

Now, a caution for U.S. country team civilian leaders — diplomats and other embassy officials need to think and act 'beyond the pavement' (see Chapter 3). Traditional diplomatic emphasis only on formal Afghan government institutions won't cut it. "Unfortunately, in state-building scenarios such as Iraq and Afghanistan, the professional experience of most policymakers is limited to brief tours in the Green Zone or Bagram. These places, while technically in-country, have absolutely no resemblance to the larger situation on the ground," says Steve Thomas.[4]

Afghan and coalition civilians and military advisors should collaborate and train together in the U.S. and in Europe to educate each other on these programs. Advisors should be familiar with embassy-sponsored, community-based programs, and how to reach up and connect to them as part of a long-term FID strategy. Interagency collaboration is best cultivated when risk is low in pre-deployment training preparation. It doesn't cost much, and the payout can be strategic.

8. Right-size our operational footprint.

Operational footprint refers to the coalition size, disposition, and quantity of the people and organizations working in Afghanistan. Our Afghan footprint has been wrong since Green Berets and other Special Operations Forces initially ousted the Taliban in early 2002. We need to right-size.

Right now we're "spit balling" arbitrary numbers between the U.S. administration, the coalition, and the military theater commanders. This is largely because of ambiguous U.S. policy. The way our diplomats and warriors are waiting for Washington to give them guidance is appalling.

Let's stop worrying so much initially about numbers of forces. Until we redefine relative stability objectives for Afghanistan (see Chapter 8), our force structure will be out of whack. Our footprint should reflect the right people in the right places. It should represent our renewed appreciation of local realities within Afghanistan, such as rural issues. Get this right, and we get Afghan stability right.

9. Focus on quality over quantity.

We should assign advisors based on local orientation and keep them coming back to Afghanistan. This is key to going local. We moved away from this after the 9/11 attacks on the U.S. We need to bring in advisors who have a stake in the country because they will return. Re-emphasize language and culture. This work requires serious, seasoned professionals who can invest their time and master their tradecraft in long-term, relative stability.

Diplomats and other civilian leaders who value status society as much as they value contract society are key. We need open-minded advisors who have wide ranges of solutions to complex problems. They must work as comfortably in a remote village with no running water as they do in an embassy. They should be catalysts who are connectors and 'utility infielders' for group problem solving.

The number and type of advisors isn't the only footprint consideration. Where you put them also matters. A well-placed, locally embedded small group of operators can often achieve more in a rural insurgency than a large military formation tied to a built-up combat outpost or urban center. More about that shortly.

10. Think and act long-term.

We desperately need to change our internal clock on Afghanistan. Afghan relative stability is going to take time — a lot of time. We have a distorted view of time that is not only unrealistic, it is dangerous to Afghanistan's future — and ours.

The last 15 years in Afghanistan have created an impatient approach to stability indicative of our Western, society-of-contract mindset.[5] We approach Afghan stability with a McDonald's drive-through mentality: "I want it fast, and I want it now!"

There is a saying modified from the Vietnam War that "the coalition didn't fight a 13-year war, it fought a one-year war, 13 times." We try to win it all on one rotation, rather than build incrementally on past gains. Experience one transition between tactical military units at any level in Afghanistan to see just how true this is. This misguided time concept comes from the most senior levels of leadership and then filters down.

Starting with the Saur Revolution in April 1978, it took over 23 years of nonstop external meddling, civil war, warlord predation, abject poverty, and a range of other instability drivers to bring Afghanistan to the point in which its civil society was degraded and exploited by al Qa'ida — ultimately prompting our intervention.

It's been another 16 years of war and instability since we arrived. That's 39 years of nonstop warfare — longer than most Afghans have been alive! In fact, many Afghans have never known relative stability in their lifetime. With this in mind, we should abandon the urgent Global War on Terror timeline of 'pressure, pursue, punish' to a more viable long-term approach of 'presence, patience, and persistence.'

Let's start managing expectations now. The mantra should be "Fifty Years of FID." It will be at least this long before we will see an Afghanistan capable of standing on its own with minimal oversight. We are fooling ourselves if we think they will be ready by the end of the Trump administration or any single administration. This is more Western delusion to suit our own misguided policy of trying to play to domestic political bases. Since our involvement in 2002, the U.S. has had a complete disregard for the damaged Afghanistan governmental capacity, lack of community resiliency, and a massive localized culture of violence.

A long-term approach places proper emphasis on relationships. Here we take the iceberg of society model and put status society relationships before contract society transactions. In an honor-based, status society like Afghanistan, this technique is essential. With a longer view, organizations and leaders are more focused on building on the success of those that went before them...and setting the next group up for success. Small gains across all stability disciplines become strategic, cumulative contributions on a long-term spectrum. Just like U.S. efforts with Colombia in the 1980s and 1990s, we should also take heart and know that persistence pays off, as it has in many other at-risk countries.

Our senior leaders need to establish a long-term stability expectation between Afghanistan and the U.S. This should be an effects-based approach, built under local realities, and not a timeline that communicates to the extremists how long they need to wait us out. Our campaign should reflect the general direction and milestones necessary to achieve relative Afghan stability. Within that context, we can go local and win big.

11. Restart VSO and embassy-sponsored, community-based stability activities.

> *"Any attempt to bring peace in Afghanistan and Pakistan's Pashtun-inhabited areas requires a social repair process to help stitch the broken society damaged by the last 40 years of war, internal conflict, external interventions, and the arrival of an extremist ideology and the resultant unbridled violence that has damaged Pashtun tribal structure."*
>
> — Dr. Khan Idris, *Jirga: The Pashtun Way of Conflict Resolution*

We need an Afghan FID strategy that orients on the aspects of a damaged rural society, not just a formal state structure. The VSO methodology can operationalize this strategy as an economy of scale effort.

The current top-down emphasis on building Afghan security capacity is ineffective. We are partnering with Afghan Security Forces at senior and regional levels. That's fine as far as it goes but the Afghan government simply can't control the rural areas where over 75 percent of Afghans live, and where violent extremists exert their unmatched influence.

One special operator explained to me as recently as May 2014 that insurgents, bristling with small arms and RPG grenade launchers, are now openly walking through bazaars and previously secured areas not far from urban centers where coalition forces are consolidating. Other discussions with my Afghan sources reveal similar increased insurgent presence in previously stable VSO areas. This is an atrocious waste of our past blood, treasure, and trust.

Some leaders dismiss these rural areas as "little t" Taliban areas. If you can't see it, it doesn't count. This is dangerous. Most national uprisings in Afghanistan have come from the rural areas, as did the planning and attack on September 11, 2001.

"Since the Soviet invasion in 1979, Afghanistan's wars have been primarily won — and lost — in rural areas," according to a January 2013 report by Special Operations in Afghanistan.[6] Yet as I write this, there is virtually no U.S. or coalition presence in the rural areas of Afghanistan where the greatest extremist safe havens lie. We have given it all back. Almost all village stability sites have been abandoned by Special Operations Forces.

Leaving the rural areas uncovered with the knowledge of their fragility and exploitation by extremists is now an unmitigated disaster for Afghanistan, and ultimately our security at home. As we focus on helping Afghans with their formal institutions, we need to also help with the status society, as we did with VSO.

Afghan Local Police (ALP) are a viable solution in select areas for grassroots security. But no one is currently advising these armed groups. We've over-loved ALP as the silver bullet solution to securing Afghan rural areas, while prematurely decoupling the responsible VSO advisory mechanism that enabled it to function effectively in the first place. "The question here is how can we make ALP an instrument of our effort to establish security and establish an organic link between the people and their government rather than something that tears it apart?" warned Henry Ensher, U.S. Department of State Senior Civilian Representative to south Afghanistan in 2010.[7]

Until these damaged communities are resilient enough to manage their local police, the program should be connected to VSO advisors. "Developing Afghan Local Police without having Special Forces at the advising level is like baking bread without using yeast," wrote Dave Phillips, former Green Beret in the CIDG program in Vietnam, and a pioneer of the VSO program. We handed over ALP way too fast — and we know it.

12. Partner with Afghan Special Forces in the rural communities.

"The other day a young boy came up to me, took me by the hand, and said 'Don't go down that road brother, there is a bomb there,'" an Afghan Special Forces sergeant told me during a Kandahar interview. "He did this because a few days before, I stopped and talked with them. Rather than push them aside like many soldiers do, I gave him a soccer ball and treated him like my little brother."[8]

This pretty much says it all.

The unruly rural areas need an Afghan security force to do three things that we are currently not preparing them for:

(1)   Be present in local areas day and night to prevent intimidation and retribution by extremists. This includes a high degree of lethality when needed, and some staying power.

(2)   Behave well when no one is looking. Even in the absence of Afghan government oversight, rural communities, police, and leaders need an example of what responsible community security behavior looks like, even in the worst of times.

(3)   Serve as a catalyst to connect formal government representatives with informal civil society members and leaders. This can be achieved through the credibility of living in the area.

The right organization for these requirements is the Afghan National Army Special Forces (ANA SF). With focused capacity building, the ANA SF are well suited to work in rural villages from the bottom-up. U.S. SOF have been training them to do this since 2010.

A few years ago, Afghan Special Forces demonstrated their potential in a west Kandahar Village Stability site. A regular Afghan Army soldier was driving a truck recklessly through a crowded area of the District Center, causing Afghan civilians to jump frantically out of the way. An ANA Special Forces team leader stopped the truck, removed the soldier from the truck, reprimanded him, took his keys and gave them to a local Noorzai tribal elder. The Afghan Special Forces captain told the elder he could return the keys when he felt satisfied the man publicly atoned for his actions and would drive safely in the future.

ANA Special Forces in rural villages were well underway in 2010–12, but then stopped as part of transition. Since they were removed from rural areas, their mission is floundering and ill defined. If we don't act to clarify their role, they will be subsumed into yet another strike force.[9]

The ANA Special Forces aren't proficient enough yet for this demanding grassroots work in rural villages. They need assistance, advice, and training — and lots of it. But there is a catch. To do this, we must be with them in the rural areas.

13. Live among them (bottom-up).

"In these undergoverned areas we can't reach from the embassy, these are the areas where special operations can add value for the long haul." This from my colleague in USAID who had worked closely with SOF for years, seeing firsthand the impact they can have in supporting host nation and country team objectives at the rural, village level.[10]

U.S. Army Special Forces and Marine Special Operations Forces, USAID Office of Transition Initiatives, and Department of State expeditionary diplomats are all well suited to advise in rough areas. Our coalition partners also have some of these capabilities. They are the right people, we just need to put them in the right places, give them the right training, the right authorities, and the right resources.

Get out of our own way!

Many of our current Afghan stability challenges are self-inflicted. "You can't do VSO from a built-up combat outpost. You can't go in half-hearted. This thing has to be done fully embedded with the villagers and living amongst them as part of their village," Captain John told me from his Kandahar VSO site.[11] He understood the connection of a marginalized Pashtun village to an inept district government. Our advisors need to have authority and resources to work with their Afghan partners in rural areas. To do this, we need to do several things to get out of our own way.

First, U.S. SOF, and ANA SF need formal authority, including congressional authority, to operate at community levels. To mobilize Afghan Special Forces to work in the rural areas, senior U.S. coalition and SOF leaders will have to engage U.S. and Afghan leadership on this issue. Traditional Foreign Internal Defense missions typically don't have provisions for this. The Afghan government will need to be convinced of the need to advise in rural areas.

Second, we should focus residual support of U.S. combat resources to this austere footprint. Whatever remains in Afghanistan — operational fires, logistics, airlift, and medical evacuation — should be oriented not just on strike missions, but on embedded advisors to ANA SF in irregular, rural stability operations.

We should also reconsider the inherent capabilities of Special Forces and other advisors to operate in austere environments. That means teaching this rugged, austere approach to ANA Special Forces as well. Remote Foreign Internal Defense with irregular forces isn't new; look at Colombian Special Forces as an example. There is also considerable SOF doctrine on how to sustain this kind of austere footprint in rough places. We may just have to knock the dust off some old manuals at the Special Forces library and bring in some old-school Green Beret mentors.

Third, we should get rid of well-meaning but risk-averse policies that preclude us from advising in rural areas. For example, there is an ISAF "Golden Hour" medical evacuation policy, which states coalition forces cannot operate beyond the one-hour reach of friendly evacuation aircraft. This policy doesn't consider the significant capability of SOF medics who can perform battlefield trauma surgery, veterinary medicine, and dentistry, and even prescribe medications. These medical capabilities are designed to operate beyond the reach of the golden hour, not within it.

Similar limitations exist for other force protection measures: Driving up-armored vehicles, wearing foreign-looking body armor, and traveling restrictions are often mission inhibiting in rural areas. All of these should be reconsidered as part of a long-term Afghan transition. It's about educating our own leaders.

U.S. Special Forces, for example, are designed for this remote work. These Green Berets can provide unparalleled medical care, construction, and engineering; a diversity of weapons training; and communications ranging from Morse code to computer networks management — all using target language and culture. However, it's amazing how many policymakers and senior strategists don't even know they have this capability at their disposal. Right now, we are too focused on drones and raids.

To be fair, Special Forces are also responsible for this lack of self-awareness, due to our self-selection away from the nuanced, indirect approach in favor of the lethal actions employed since the War on Terror began. Advisors need to get back to their roots and find their 'inner Lawrence.'

I understand I am implying greater risk for these warrior-advisors. I wish I were wrong, and drone strikes alone would get it done. But living among locals is decisive for achieving relative stability in undergoverned areas.

Shadows on the graveyard...

If we don't change our current course, my findings from my last assessment trip to Afghanistan will come back to haunt us. "History casts a long shadow on those who don't value Afghanistan's history," claimed longtime filmmaker and student of Afghanistan, John Burroughs.[12]

The graveyard of empires runs long and deep from such callous arrogance.

But unlike the previous residents in the Afghan graveyard, our withdrawal is not the end, but the beginning of something even more sinister. The storm gathers as violent extremists, including ISIS, return to the shattered Afghan villages and an emboldened enemy readies its next battle plans.

Launching violence from these Afghan safe havens, they will come for us again. Taking action to implement the strategic points within this chapter, if we are persistent, will defeat violent extremists in Afghanistan and improve our safety at home.

Chapter Highlights

- *Leaving the rural areas uncovered with the knowledge of their fragility and exploitation by extremists is now an unmitigated disaster for Afghanistan, and ultimately our security at home.*

- *To achieve relative stability in Afghanistan we need to adopt a long-term, small-footprint, Remote Area Foreign Internal Defense (FID) strategy.*

- *This whole-of-nation approach, led by the U.S. country team, includes U.S. and Afghan Special Operations Forces advising regular security forces and indigenous clans to achieve relative stability in a country largely dominated by informal clan society.*

- *Our meek withdrawal from Afghanistan empowers our extremist enemies with spiritual momentum. They will come for us again. Our actions in Afghanistan will determine the future of our safety at home.*

- *The 13 points in this chapter are applicable in at-risk areas beyond Afghanistan, like Iraq and Syria.*

Chapter 12

No Respite: Islamist Violent Extremists in the Homeland

"So resolve upon your plan and [call upon] your associates. Then let not your plan be obscure to you. Then carry it out upon me and do not give me respite."

— Quran, verse 10:71

The Pulse nightclub, Orlando, Florida, June 12, 2016

"I pledge allegiance to Abu Bakr al Baghdadi. This is a shout-out to my homeboys the Tsarnov brothers. This is for all the people killed by U.S. bombs in Syria."

As U.S.–born Omar Mateen continued his cell phone rant with a 911 dispatcher, dozens of his victims lay dead or suffering on the blood-stained floor of the popular discotheque.

Outside, federal and local police special response teams were stacked at their designated points of entry, anxiously waiting the "GO" signal to mount an assault and stop the bloodshed. But not until nearly four hours after the shooting started would those teams finally get the call, and in short order the terrorist Mateen was dead. But not before he had shot 102 people; 49 killed and 53 wounded. He fired a total of 110 bullets during his murderous killing spree.

Just one hour from where my kids go to school — 20 minutes from where hundreds of thousands of families come to experience the Disney and Universal theme park magic — ISIS had come to Florida. With this murderous act, amplified by Mateen's own use of social media during the killing siege, the cumulative effects of a violent Islamist extremist splattered blood onto some fresh virgin fabric of American society — an LGBT nightclub. ISIS had done what al Qa'ida could not or would not do: they had brought the war to Main Street, USA, just like they had already done in Western Europe.

"Blessed Battle of Manchester: A New Lesson for Tyrant Crusader States." This was the headline in an ISIS weekly newspaper just hours after a suicide bombing attack at an Ariana Grande pop concert in Manchester, England. The article bragged: "Protected by the sea, they have long relied on isolating themselves. A soldier from the Islamic State has unleashed terror throughout their country."

This ISIS media piece brings out two critical components about these ISIS attacks on local entertainment venues:

First, ISIS views locations like Orlando and Manchester as "battlefields" in a military campaign, while we continue to evaluate them as random crime scenes.

Second, ISIS designates its surrogates who carry out these deadly attacks in the West as "Soldiers of the Islamic State," while we continue to refer them as "lone wolves." These seemingly insignificant distinctions are exactly the gaps that can diminish our preparation and responses and bring great harm to our people here at home and throughout Western Europe.

Since writing the first edition of this book, the game has changed again. So much has shifted on the terrorist scene, in fact, that I felt compelled to add another chapter to this abridged citizen guide for the express purpose of getting in front of the enemy before they can burrow even deeper into our homeland.

The enduring drumbeat of violent Islamist extremists continues. But the enemy's march tempo has quickened to a double-time. Simultaneously, the top-down, misguided Western style of war against this asymmetric threat accelerates as we continually spend exorbitant amounts of blood and treasure with nearly no enduring effect on our foe. The vulnerabilities and opportunities I highlighted in *Game Changers* have never been more valid and timeless, but we are running out of time.

My predictions of the enemy's behavior — and ours — have manifested with alarming levels of violence in the West, and even in the U.S., much faster than I ever imagined. The reason was unexpected, but simple.

ISIS: Islamic State in Iraq and Syria, or Daesh

I'm shifting my focus from al Qa'ida to ISIS, which is accomplishing its wartime objectives far more efficiently and effectively than al Qa'ida ever dreamed of, and it is kicking our collective Western asses in the process. If you are concerned about ISIS, this chapter is for you — the citizen, the law enforcement officer, the local leader. What should you know about ISIS? What can be done?

Regardless of what former U.S. Commander in Chief Barack Obama has said, ISIS represents a much higher, existential threat than any other force in the bad guy inventory. They are no longer just "over there" in remote terror camps, swinging on monkey bars, and planning the occasional high-profile attack on high-visibility targets in the U.S. ISIS supporters who are also often perfectly legal U.S. citizens or green card holders download backpack bomb recipes while surfing the Internet at Starbucks and practice their shooting sprees at local indoor shooting ranges.

The American battlefield has shifted from the Pentagon and the World Trade Center to health centers in San Bernardino, California, recruiting stations in Chattanooga, Tennessee, and nightclubs in Orlando, Florida. Young people are now a common target, as in 'pre-Wall' Israel.

What does this rapid emergence of a new brand of terrorism at home mean to you as an individual, as a citizen? What does it mean to your family and the community where you live? What does it mean to law enforcement? Local politicians and community leaders? What does it mean to our kids? What does it mean to our future?

As with the rest of the book, our friends in Western Europe should find extreme relevance in this chapter as well. Sadly, ISIS is entrenched even deeper in your ancient neighborhoods and communities, and your battle against ISIS throughout Europe will be costly. And if we fail to learn from your lessons, your reality will soon be ours here in the United States.

At the risk of getting overly technical, ISIS is willing to do violent shit to us in ways that no other enemy on the planet is willing to do. As I'll show later in this chapter, their ideological will — their commitment to a terrifying master narrative — combined with their ever-growing capacity for local strikes in the places where we live, shop, and eat put them in a whole new terror category.

Orlando was only the beginning. ISIS is just getting warmed up. To understand why the future is increasingly dangerous, we need to see what's changed. Let's look at what's bringing this troubling reality to our front door.

What's changed?

ISIS emerged from the ashes of al Qa'ida in Iraq (AQI) and its former brutal terror leader, the Jordanian ex-convict Abu Zarqawi. They have exploited the U.S. departure from Iraq in 2011 and the heavy-handedness of the Iraqi government to eclipse al Qa'ida as the preeminent global Islamist terror group. They have gained and held territory in Syria and Iraq now known as the caliphate, which al Qa'ida was unable to do. And they have created a master narrative and global following based on ruthless apocalyptic violence that has escalated terrorism in our homeland to an unprecedented level.

ISIS is unleashing more attacks on the West than any Islamist terror group in history. In Western Europe, after decades of unchecked immigration policies, ISIS uses 'stealth jihad,' known as *Hijrah* (meaning migration, like that done by the prophet Mohammad from Mecca to Medina to begin the Muslim era), to exploit these marginalized communities, by hiding in plain site within those neighborhoods, and launching complex attacks from them before disappearing right back into them.

Note: In every one of these local attacks, there was some knowledge of the impending terrorist action among the perpetrators' inner circles of family and neighbors — that is, before the attacks occurred. This becomes very important later when we talk about community engagement and going local.

Terror attacks have gone from Wall Street to Main Street. World Trade Center–type attacks have given way to local attacks on the places where we live every day, such as parades, restaurants, and festivals. Children and their mothers are now the targets, not collateral damage.

Centralized planning with carefully controlled execution by highly trained operatives who are smuggled into the target area has been supplanted by decentralized execution by surrogates who are inspired by ISIS' centralized narrative and broad targeting guidance, often provided through glossy magazines like *Dabiq*. This is occurring just as unprecedented political, ethnic, religious, and social divisions within the United States have eroded trust and social capital to create a climate of animosity and conflict that ISIS can drive a truck through — the kind of truck they mow people down with.

"You drop bombs that cost $250,000," says ISIS in its propaganda video *No Respite*. "Meanwhile, our surrogates kill you with 50-cent bullets." ISIS tells us exactly what they intend to do to us. But when they follow through, we dismiss it, allowing them to burrow even deeper into the local fabric of our society while political correctness from U.S. politicians, senior law enforcement officials, and media pundits misrepresents high-impact terror attacks, like the one in Orlando, as "lone-wolf" crimes by fringe elements. In fact, the FBI omitted all of Mateen's references to Islam and ISIS in his 911 call from the Pulse nightclub until it was publicly pressured to release the full recording.

Other politically correct arguments label ISIS attacks as a problem of 'gun control.' This argument persists although some of the worst ISIS attacks have occurred in France and the UK, where almost no citizens own guns, and while many Americans and other Westerners have become indifferent or inattentive to the emerging ISIS terror threat. Citizens are also blissfully tolerant of the intellectually dishonest political correctness and Attention Deficit Disorder (ADD) behavior of media reporting when terror events occur. A few hours of reporting on horrific events and the media moves on to talking about the Kardashians or other non-news events.

Why should we care?

Terrorism has taken on a new level of danger in America. Terrorism has now expanded its violence to become horrorism.

Terrorism is the preferred tool for al Qa'ida, defined as the use of violence on civilian populations to achieve a political outcome. But horrorism is the preferred tool for ISIS. Horrorism is the application of horrific, in-your-face violence at local levels to achieve compliance and unadulterated fear, and ultimately it results in a desire for unmitigated revenge among its victims.

ISIS is hell-bent on showing up the 'has-beens' of al Qa'ida they are the new 'big dog' on the block. They do this by making 9/11 seem like a walk in the park, in an effort to paralyze our citizens with fear locally, and draw us into a deeper war strategically.

ISIS horrorism represents a much greater risk to ordinary Americans for unmitigated, interpersonal violence by violent Islamist extremists as we go about our daily lives. A recent Gallup poll indicates that "38 percent of Americans are less willing to attend large events due to terrorism." This is even higher than the 32 percent of Americans who felt that way right after 9/11 in 2001.[1]

Strategically, ISIS also poses a much greater threat to the U.S. than al Qa'ida in terms of suckering us into a quagmire military campaign as a response to its incessant over-the-top acts of violence on the most vulnerable elements of our society.

How is ISIS different from al Qa'ida?

First, where they are similar: Both claim to believe in some version of a prophecy that re-establishes the Islamic Caliphate, creates an epic battle between crusaders and holy Islamic warriors, and ultimately ushers in judgment day.

Now, the differences:

- One of the major differences between al Qa'ida and ISIS is urgency. ISIS has convinced its followers the time for the prophecy and the end of days is <u>right now</u>, not in some far off, nebulous time as cautiously advanced by al Qa'ida senior leaders like Zawahiri.

- This right-now mindset drives ISIS to manufacture a holy war. They want to draw in crusaders and apostates to an epic battle based on their end-of-days prophecy. Even their magazine, *Dabiq*, is named after the foreseen location of the battle of Armageddon in Islam.

- ISIS religious courts issue fatwas that justify, and in fact, encourage horrorism — any acts of audacious violence that instill fear and mobilize action toward their efforts to draw the West into their manufactured holy war. Beheading, burning alive, sex slavery, and harvesting organs from live humans; nothing is off the table for a group that even al Qa'ida thinks is out of control.

- ISIS is all in. They eclipse even al Qa'ida commitment in their belief in their ideology. Belief in the end-of-days prophecy runs as deeply with senior leader Abu Bakr al-Baghdadi as it did with the lowest surrogate, Omar Mateen, in Orlando.

- ISIS markets its violence masterfully through digital media and strategic messaging. Violence sells within their following — and business is good.

- ISIS is more adept at exploiting the social divisions within the West than al Qa'ida. They pick the scabs off festering U.S. domestic social wounds like racism, political corruption, and even military suicides, and then exploit them through digital media propaganda.

- ISIS goes local. They don't need the big spectacular attack. Quite the contrary: they want you scared, personally. They want you peeking out of your blinds, afraid to turn on the television, and unwilling to go out in public. They attack everyday citizens with knives, trucks, and suicide vests. In spring 2017, ISIS published in their *Rumiyah* magazine a step-by-step guide on how to purchase a large truck and maximize its lethality when running people over with it. Their goal is to invoke raw fear at a local level and elicit visceral collective revenge against them at a strategic level. Here is why:

  - Without an infidel army at the door, the prophecy doesn't happen, and followers will slip away. A sizeable Western response to their persistent attacks is the only way their followers will continue to believe the prophecy can be realized.

  - They tell us this in no uncertain terms. "Bring it on," they bark at us in their propaganda video, "show us no respite." We just choose to ignore it, just as the West ignored Hitler's acts of savagery.

What can be done?

It doesn't have to be this way. The game changers recommended in this book are more relevant than ever.

First, we must recognize ISIS' increased ideological desire to bring violence into our lives at a local community level and to draw us strategically into a manufactured holy war. To ignore that mindset is dangerous and will allow them to grow stronger with each passing day.

This requires an informed citizenry. Yes, you. Our politicians have made it abundantly clear that they are not going to get deep on this enemy — that they will either ignore them through political correctness, or bomb the hell out of them with the tired 'rinse and repeat' strategy that's been used unsuccessfully since the Bush administration.

It's up to you. An informed citizenry is our best chance to change the game against violent extremists here at home. We need an activated citizenry who can put political pressure on our senior leaders. This can create meaningful policy and strategy to change the game and defeat ISIS. Targeting of ISIS and al Qa'ida abroad and arresting their followers in our homeland must remain a high priority; however, the local tactics abroad and at home, should be done within the context of a community-based engagement strategy. We need to demand this of our leaders.

The Game Changer of going local for empowered communities is essential as an antibody to ISIS, but now, we need these 'antibody communities' right here in the U.S. and throughout Western Europe. This means locating and empowering resilient leaders within these communities who are willing to take a stand and root out violent extremists. This will require local politicians and law enforcement officials to pick up Chapter 7, get surrounded, and meet people in these at-risk communities where the violent perpetrators are located. You can do the same things in your role as a citizen. Reach out. Connect to the communities around you.

Our national politicians need to stop fomenting identity politics and in-group/out-group behavior. Instead, we need our political leaders and senior leaders at institutional levels to start restoring trust and bridging the numerous social divides within the U.S. This includes redefining our collective national identity to rally Americans beyond their immediate in-groups and stand against the violent extremism that is surely coming our way.

Both national and local political leaders need to foster an environment of honest internal discourse about ISIS and violent Islamist extremist realities. This should include resilient leaders from marginalized Islamic communities. And we should shun the political correctness of muzzled dialogue to openly talk about the vulnerabilities, along with the opportunities we face as a nation in defeating this existential threat of violent Islamist extremism.

We must restore an emphasis on community policing throughout America. This is a timeless approach to not only law enforcement, but also community engagement and empowerment. And it bears repeating that an engaged community — a community that has a positive relationship with the state — is a powerful antibody to ISIS. Whereas a marginalized community, often created through top-down, intelligence-based law enforcement and targeting, can serve as an accelerant for ISIS and other outside agitators. We must remember that internal warfare develops where governance fails.

Law enforcement and their controlling politicians must re-examine the model for analyzing domestic terror attacks to recognize ISIS surrogate strikes in our homeland for what they are, the new preferred method for ISIS to strike us where we live, and not define these horrorism events as random, "lone-wolf" attacks.

Strategists should vastly change the way we prepare for future ISIS and al Qa'ida attacks at home and recognize ISIS' ideological preference for over-the-top local violence, and their desire to piss us off and draw us in even deeper by attacking or expelling Muslims. We must ask ourselves, how will they try to emotionally draw us in to their manufactured holy war, and how can we avoid making things worse?

Everyone must look deeply at protecting our kids, our local communities, and our infrastructure. We can better protect our freedom as Americans with fewer top-down federal actions that create more problems than solutions and more bottom-up, local engagement and community policing.

Parting thoughts...

Failure to change the game on fighting ISIS here at home could result in the unthinkable. Left unchecked, ISIS will come for our kids just as they did in Manchester, and as suicide bombers did in Tel Aviv before the Wall stopped their infiltration. Killing our children is the best way to draw us into the fight they want us to be drawn into, in order to fulfill the ancient prophecy that binds their followers to them.

Recently, I was training a local Florida sheriff's agency on ISIS activities, and as I started talking about ISIS' desire for end-of-days and goading us into a holy war, several of the deputies were rolling their eyes and smirking at this seemingly outlandish warning. Less than two weeks later, at the Ariana Grande concert in Manchester, little 8-year-old Saffie Roussos and 22 other victims were killed by an ISIS suicide bomber, and 220 people in all received medical treatment as a result of the blast.

Now ISIS is calling for more of the same.

Their operating logic is simple — and right in line with their prophetic methodology. Yet our preferred Western way of war, our growing internal loss of trust with one another and social divisions, and our continually debilitating political correctness prevent us from seeing what they tell us they intend to do.

ISIS wants a fight — and they want it with us. To wake the sleeping giant, they will come for the thing that will piss us off the most. Our kids. Failure to act and get in front of this growing threat could have catastrophic effects on our nation and our people. For the sake of our kids, and the future of our country, we have to change the game on how we fight them at home, as much as we must change how we fight them abroad.

More intensely driven than al Qa'ida ever was, the audacity of violence and rapid pace of execution that ISIS demonstrates in the U.S. doesn't give us much time.

Chapter 13

Conclusion

Wisdom is not knowledge. Wisdom is understanding knowledge. You can gain wisdom by observing the folly of others, and concluding there must be a better way.

— Timothy G. Bax, *Who Will Teach the Wisdom*

9/11 Memorial, Ground Zero, New York, New York, July 2014

Overwhelming. That's the only word that comes to mind as I tried to gather my thoughts. I was sitting under a shade tree. It was not a big shade tree. It hadn't had many years to grow. Nothing grew here for a long time after that sad September day.

This was exactly where I needed to be to close this story out. I chose to write the "Bypassing the Graveyard" chapter in Afghanistan, and I chose to write the conclusion of my book here at Ground Zero. Despite all the analytical rigor required for this project, I needed to get my mind right and close out from a place of service and call to higher purpose. I had to be right here — where it all started.

Like many other battlefields I've visited in my life, there was a false normalcy at the 9/11 Memorial in Manhattan. But despite the beauty of the new World Trade superstructure, the glass museum, and the cascading reflecting pools that mark the two footprints of where the towers once stood, the horror was still just below the surface.

It wasn't that long ago that terror delivered by Islamist violent extremists fell upon these New York streets like the volcano of Pompeii. I looked up from my laptop to see hundreds of people milling about. Many had their cell phones out taking selfies in front of the various monument structures, laughing and enjoying the beautiful New York summer weather.

A young woman caught my attention. She was standing near the North reflecting pool. I noticed her because she was crying — a lot. She was looking down at the spot on the memorial wall where the 9/11 victims' names were inscribed. At one particular name.

I had seen this kind of pain before. Too much. It was in the eyes of Staff Sergeant Victor's mom as she kept screaming "Por que (why)?! Por que (why)?!" until her voice failed her, and she could only mouth the words to me after we buried her son. It was in the tears of Sergeant First Class Chris' 12-year-old boy as the bagpipes played "Amazing Grace" and the sadness lifted us up together and carried us hand-in-hand, in bitter sadness, in the funeral march to his dad's gravesite.

Today, despite the thousands of people, this woman's familiar mourning was all I could see on this hallowed ground. She traced the name on the side of the reflecting pool with her index finger over and over as she softly spoke to it. The pain floated from her silent words right into my chest.

It hit me like a semi-truck as I closed my laptop and put my head in my hands. Strangers or not, I didn't dare let anyone see this loss of emotion. Memories of my Ranger buddy Cliff Patterson, killed in the Pentagon, came flooding in. Memories from the weeks after 9/11 of the young kids and spouses desperately posting pictures of their mom, dad, husband, or wife on any spare wall they could find.

Thousands of miles away, so many of my friends had died in Afghanistan. Memorial after memorial, over the years, where "Taps" played and the tears flowed freely. Images came back to me of never-ending hand salutes to makeshift memorials of an erect rifle, worn-out desert boots, dog tags, a Green Beret, and a photo of another lost Brother.

My final flood of emotion was the ice water running through my veins as my oldest son told me not long ago that he wanted to be a Green Beret like his Dad. While immensely proud of him, I couldn't help but worry that he would fall in on the same mistakes we failed to learn. This made my investment in changing how we play this deadly game all the more important to me.

Going local and changing the game is immensely personal to me. It's not some academic exercise or policy pontification. It's about adapting and responding to our reality so that we can protect our families and our homeland. You either believe that or you don't.

What's at stake

Many folks just want to ignore the threat of violent extremism. Lots of Americans are thinking, "Enough with the terror talk! We are done with this war. No one cares. Osama bin Laden is dead, and with him, al Qa'ida.

The former Obama administration made this abundantly clear. We are pulling out of Afghanistan. Our men and women are coming home. It's time to focus on the economy and on getting back to normal."

Unfortunately, ISIS has now reared its ugly head in a very big way.

Left unchecked, the unmatched violence of these extremists will shatter our stability at home. They are coming after us at a horrifying community level. And we will never be the same once these events start to happen.

We have a choice to make.

We can choose to change the game, or we can choose to stay on our current path.

Choice 1: This book has laid out a path for changing the game. The outcome if we change the game is clear. At-risk areas will see resiliency in formerly undergoverned areas that will allow them to handle their own affairs. Their willingness to work with the government will increase. The balance of relative stability will improve to a level that doesn't require U.S. presence. Violent extremists and criminal groups will become irrelevant and much less capable of projecting violence on our homeland.

Choice 2: If we stay on the current path, we will continue to support corrupt and incompetent governments in pushing their power top-down onto marginalized populations, who already distrust them. Staying on the current path means a continued emphasis on body-count warfare, drone strikes, and night raids as singular lethal solutions to civil society problems, in spite of invoking tribal revenge against us. If we stay on the current path, we will accept bureaucratic parochialism and be much less likely to collaborate for more relevant solutions with those outside our immediate circles. And finally, staying on the current path means letting our enemy define our master narrative and tell the good stories.

The probable outcomes of not changing the game are unchecked expansion of extremist ideology, unacceptable levels of violence at home, and potential fiscal insolvency. This will result in us being pulled deeper into the global struggle than we already are.

Not easy

What I am proposing is difficult. It goes against the grain of our conventional wisdom. I understand the dangers and concerns of working among clans and tribalism. As a freedom-loving American, a proud son of U.S.

civil servants, and grandchild of the Appalachian Scots-Irish clans, I have seen firsthand the wonder and brilliance of a constitution-based government that embraces the rule of law and the freedom of the individual...I am a fan and a tireless defender of it.

I have voluntarily served my country for almost 23 years as a career soldier. I've also been blessed by the fruits of capitalism as an entrepreneur. I have been able to thrive in a society that values individualism. I have personally and professionally excelled without paying required patronage to my group or homage to my clan as part of my success. I would never have been able to do that in many of the places in which I worked as a Green Beret, including Afghanistan.

The world will likely be a better place when free men, protected by the rule of law, walk upon all the rough areas where clans now reign. Unfortunately, we have a long way to go. Islamist violent extremism stands directly in the path of free individuals. I believe that empowering status societies to reclaim their local legitimacy, rather than smothering them from above, while simultaneously working with partner governments, is ultimately the best way to reduce violent extremism's threat to civil society and the global economy.

These game changers are not designed to raise their own private militias or to pursue a personal agenda. Rather, they are a prescription for stable governance in rough places. For now, that's all we get. But in many cases — it's enough. Governance, which connects status and contract society, often starts locally. Advisors must win the trust of community members, and then in the time of these locals — not ours — patiently walk them back into the arms of a government that must be sincerely ready to receive them and embrace them. From Ferguson to the FATA, it's the only way to repair damaged trust exploited by extremists, agitators, and criminals.

What tomorrow brings

Most of you know we need to change the game, but it won't be easy. There are entrenched advocates who have no patience for anything new. Others see these Game Changers as even more destabilizing than the current method, yet often they have no new solutions themselves. To move forward, we'll have to get over our own Western biases at every leadership level and not let organizational parochialism get in the way.

Others will resist changing the game because they see these suggestions as destabilizing or too narrowly focused. Some will view this as an effort to revitalize the "VSO era" of Afghanistan, and thus not see that most of the Game Changer recommendations are addressing much bigger stability issues, collaboration and narratives.

Even those who disagree with this approach, and some will, are entitled to the honest rendering of who we are and what we're about. Over-communicating through an honest dialogue and transparent framework is the best way. I learned this teaching bottom-up stability at the Foreign Service Institute, USDA, and other organizations. We are often closer on these issues than we think.

We just don't talk enough.

We admittedly don't have all the answers here. In fact, we're still learning every day. There is tremendous value in acknowledging we don't know, and seeking knowledge from a place of humility and learning. There is a tendency to wait until you have a foolproof methodology, quantifiable metrics to back it up, and then — and only then — do you publish recommendations to the skeptical audience that waits. I would like nothing better than to work on this framework toward perfection, but time is one luxury we don't have.

We need people to unify around a game-changing methodology that works. These true believers are the junior- to mid-level leaders of today. They may not be in charge yet, but they will be soon. It may take five to 10 years for these future senior leaders to move to positions of influence, but they will get there. And when they do, this book and the network behind it will be there for them.

If old farts like me at senior levels read this and take it to heart, that's great, too. Realization by unbelievers and entrenched traditionalists will accelerate an inescapable reality of the strategic benefits of going local that is evolving — and their conversion will accelerate our safety at home.

It took us a long time to figure some key things out in Afghanistan, only to forget them all over again.

Shortly before I finished this project, I was doing another guest lecture with MBA students about negotiations in high-stakes situations and the bottom-up lessons from Afghanistan. After the lecture was over, two young men came up to talk with me. They introduced themselves and told me they were from Ukraine.

"What you said today about weak governments and fragile communities exploited by extremists is as much about our country as it is Afghanistan," one of them told me. "Our government is as much the enemy as the extremists. Their top-down approach isn't working and the people have lost all faith and trust in everything." He looked down with sadness. "Even my family is torn over this. They live in rebel-held territory and we are split right down the middle. This bottom-up approach is the only way. This is how it has to be, and our generation will be the ones to do it."[1]

The right people are out there now, and they are ready to move. The choice is clear — we have to go local and change the game to defeat violent extremists. For the sake of our future, and that of our children, I pray we make the right choice now.

De Oppresso Liber

(Free the Oppressed)

NOTES

PART I: DEFINING THE GAME

Chapter 1: Introduction

1. Neta C. Crawford and Catherine Lutz, *Costs of War*, Brown University Watson Institute for International Studies, http://www.costsofwar.org.
2. Shan Carter and Amanda Cox, "9/11: The Reckoning — One 9/11 Tally: 3 Trillion" *New York Times*, September 8, 2011, http://www.nytimes.com/interactive/2011/09/08/us/sept-11-reckoning/cost-graphic.html.
The breakdown on post-attack U.S. expenses was very detailed in this report. Toll and physical damage: $55 billion; economic impact: $123 billion; Homeland Security–related costs: $589 billion; war funding–related costs: $1,659 billion; and future war and veterans care: $867 billion.
3. Walter Russell Mead, "The Evolving Terror Threat," *The Wall Street Journal*, March 4, 2013, http://www.wsj.com/articles/SB1000142412788732382950457 8272033024365110.

Chapter 2: Why We Are Losing

1. Joel Gehrke, "Terrorists Handbook," *National Review Online*, August 29, 2014, http://www.nationalreview.com/article/386728terrorists-handbook-joel-gehrke.
2. *Encyclopedia Britannica*, http://brittannica.com/EBchecked/topic89139.caliphate (accessed May 16, 2014).
3. Dr. Phil Williams, "Alternative Governance in a World Without Order," lecture to Threat Day audience, Washington, D.C., January 9, 2015.
4. David Kilcullen, *Out of the Mountains* (Oxford University Press, 2013).
5. Michael F. Scheuer, "Al-Qaeda in the Islamic Maghreb (AQIM): Using crime to advance Salafist goals, secure safe havens, and acquire international reach," Tribal Analysis Center, January 2015, http://www.tribalanalysiscenter.com/Research-Completed.html
6. "New 'Manifesto' Shows al-Qaeda Learning from Mistakes," *ICSR Insight*, http://www.icsr.info, February 15, 2013.

Chapter 3: Where the Pavement Ends

1. Dr. Thomas Barfield and Neamatollah Nojumi, "Bringing More Effective Governance to Afghanistan: 10 Pathways to Stability," *Middle East Policy* 4 (Winter 2010): 3.
2. Agnieszka Flak, "Electricity only reaches one in three Afghans," Reuters, January 9, 2012.
3. *CIA World Factbook*, https://www.cia.gov/library/publications/the-world-factbook/fields/2097.html.

4. Barfield and Nojumi, "Bringing More Effective Governance to Afghanistan," p. 3.

5. Mark S. Weiner, *The Rule of the Clan* (New York: Farrar, Straus and Giroux, 2013). In this definition of "liberal," Weiner refers to societies committed to the values necessary to sustain our individualist way of life. I will use this definition of liberal society or liberal democracy throughout the book.

6. Casey Garret Johnson, "Afghan Islamic Courts: A Pre-Taliban System with Post-2014 Potential?" *New York Times*, April 17, 2013, http://atwar.blogs.nytimes.com/2013/04/17afghan-islamic-courts-a-pre-taliban-system-with-post-2014-potential/.

7. Interview with Dr. Ted Callahan, Subject Matter Expert for Northern Afghanistan and Cultural Advisor to Special Operations Joint Task Force – Afghanistan, Kabul, June 2014.

8. Barfield and Nojumi, "Bringing More Effective Governance to Afghanistan," 3.

9. "Rural Development and Counter-insurgency, A Case Study," FAF Development, Kandahar Afghanistan (2009), 8–9.

10. Weiner, *The Rule of the Clan*, 10. Weiner credits the 19th-century British scholar Henry Maine for defining societies of status and societies of contract. This framework is used throughout my book.

11. Allan Dafoe and Devin Caughey, "Honor and War: Using Southern Presidents to Identify Reputational Effects in International Conflict," 5http://citation.allacademic.com/meta/p_mla_apa_research_citation/4/9/9/1/4/pages499145/p499145-5.php.

12. Haji Lala (name changed), director of Afghan NGO, personal interview with the author, Savannah, Georgia, October 2012.

13. MRRD Deputy Minister Tariq Ismati, personal interview with the author, Savannah, Georgia, October 2012.

14. Ibid.

15. Mohammed Nabi (name changed to protect against retribution), Alikozai elder in North Kandahar Province, personal interview with the author.

16. Haji Lala, personal interview with the author, December 2012.

17. International Crisis Group, "Afghanistan: The Problem of Pashtun Alienation," *Asia Report* 62 (August 5, 2003), 6.

18. Dr. David Ellis, "Afghans have forgotten how to farm," USSOCOM Academic Week training program, Fort Bragg, North Carolina, June 2011.

19. It is during this era that much of our understanding of current Afghan realities and challenges becomes blurred. For example, we associate Arbakai (village security forces) with warlords. This is simply historically inaccurate.

20. Dr. Seth Jones, USSOCOM briefing, May 2011.

21. Personal interview with tribal leader and former Kabul national security staff, and cultural advisor (name protected to prevent retribution) to Special Operations Forces, Kabul, Afghanistan, May 20, 2014. One of the most knowledgeable men I ever worked with on Afghan tribal dynamics and local realities. He possessed unmatched skills at connecting formal and outlying society across the country and across all ethnic lines.

Chapter 4: Square Tank in a Round Jirga

1. Tom Coghlan, "The Taliban in Helmand: An oral history," in *Decoding the New Taliban*, ed. Antonio Giustozzi (Oxford: Oxford University Press, 2012).

2. Interview with Dr. Ted Callahan, Subject Matter Expert for Northern Afghanistan and Cultural Advisor to Special Operations Joint Task Force – Afghanistan, Kabul, June 2014.

3. I base this observation on two consecutive tours as a battalion and group SOF Operations officer in Afghanistan. I personally prepared and developed attrition metrics for commanders while in Afghanistan and upon return on numerous occasions.

4. I identified this report through another report: Stephen Carter and Kate Clark, "No Shortcut to Stability," Chatham House, December 15, 2010, http://www.chathamhouse.org/publications/papers/view/109545. The authors highlighted a TLO study on night raids: OSI and the Liaison Office (2010), "Strangers at the Door; Night Raids by International Forces Lose Hearts and Minds of Afghans," Kabul Open Society Institute/Tribal Liaison Office, Kabul, 2010, 8.

5. Every Special Operations force is different; people often get them confused. The forte of U.S. Army Special Forces, also known as Green Berets, is typically to work by, with, and through indigenous populations to achieve indirect strategic effects in support of U.S. strategy. Early in Operation Enduring Freedom, just after the attacks of 9-11, Special Forces did this with members of the Northern Alliance and other resistance groups to overthrow the Taliban in Afghanistan. This type of mission is the bread and butter of Special Forces and is known as Unconventional Warfare. However, after hostile regimes are overthrown, Special Forces usually transition into their other primary mission set, known as Foreign Internal Defense. Once again, Green Berets work by, with, and through indigenous forces but this time it is to stabilize friendly governments against insurgency and lawlessness. It involves training, advising, and assisting regular forces like host nation army and police as well as irregular forces like the Afghan Local Police. For a range of reasons, Special Forces self-selected out of this mission in favor of the more kinetic man-hunting mission and passed it off to the conventional military, namely the National Guard. They even gave up Title 10 Authority, the budgetary authority empowered by Congress to resource host nation forces when training and advising them. When working with Afghan counterparts in OEF, Special Forces had to rely on National Guard Embedded Tactical Trainers (ETTs) anytime host nation funding was required. This was self-neutering at its worst in favor of the more attractive man-hunting missions.

6. Rory Stewart, "Afghanistan: 'A Shocking Indictment,'" review of *No Good Men Among the Living*, by Anand Gopal, *The New York Review of Books*, November 6, 2014.

7. Antonio Giustozzi, *Koran, Kalashnikov, and Laptop: The Neo-Taliban Insurgency in Afghanistan* (New York: Columbia University Press, 2008), 97.

8. Giustozzi, *Koran, Kalashnikov, and Laptop*, 214. Note: "the right people" was in quotes by Giustozzi in this excerpt as the group identified by the U.S. and U.K. development officials.

9. Dr. Khan Idris, "Jirgas: Pashtun Participatory Governance," Tribal Analysis Center, Williamsburg, Virginia, 2009, 11.

10. Personal interview with MRRD Deputy Minister Tariq Ismati, Savannah, Georgia, October 2012.

11. Personal interview with Dr. Callahan, Kabul, June 2014.

12. Dr. Thomas Barfield and Neamatollah Nojumi, "Bringing More Effective Governance to Afghanistan: 10 Pathways to Stability," *Middle East Policy* 4 (Winter 2010): 1.

13. Carter and Clark, "No Shortcut to Stability," http://www.chathamhouse .org/publications/papers/view/109545.

14. Giustozzi, *Koran, Kalashnikov, and Laptop,* 163.

PART II: CHANGING THE GAME

Chapter 5: Finding Lawrence

1. Joseph Collins, "The Rise and Fall of Major Jim Gant," *War on the Rocks*, April 15, 2014. In the article on Major Gant cited by Collins, I stumbled upon this quote by Andrew Exum: "I just don't see how the U.S. can back a strategy that is predicated upon being implemented by geniuses." http://warontherocks.com/2014/04/ the-rise-and-fall-of-major-jim-gant/.

2. Linda Robinson, *One Hundred Victories: Special Ops and the Future of American Warfare* (New York: Public Affairs, New York 2013), 263.

3. Ride-along field research with Chief Kelly McMillin of the Salinas Police Department, Salinas, California, October 2014.

4. Ann Scott Tyson, *American Spartan: The Promise, the Mission, and the Betrayal of Special Forces Major Jim Gant* (New York: Harper Collins, 2014).

5. This is the line the Verizon Guy always uses on the commercials as he expands his network.

6. David Ignatius, "Drawing down, but still projecting power," *The Washington Post*, March 29, 2013.

7. Personal interview with Captain Trey, former Arghandab VSO Commander and originator of that site. Interview conducted at Fort Walton Beach, Florida, February 2014.

8. U.S. Army, USMC, and U.S. SOC, "Winning the Clash of Wills," Strategic Landpower White Paper, 2013, http://www.arcic.army.mil/app_Documents/Strategic -Landpower-White-Paper-28OCT2013.pdf.

9. Personal interview with Major Gene, Fort Bragg, North Carolina, April 2014.

10. Pauline Baker, "Unraveling Afghanistan," *The American Interest*, December 19, 2013, http://www.the-american-interest.com/articles/2013/12/19 unraveling-afghanistan/.

Chapter 6: Game Changer Framework

1. Human Rights Watch, *Just Don't Call It a Militia: Impunity, Militias, and the "Afghan Local Police"* (New York: Human Rights Watch, September 2011), http://www.hrw.org/sites/default/files/reports/afghanistan0911webwcover.pdf.

2. Ibid., 6.

3. Ibid., 5.

4. COL Donald Bolduc, "Report on Progress Toward Security and Stability in Afghanistan," U.S. Department of Defense, October 2011; also COL Donald Bolduc, "Impact of Pulling U.S. SOF from Afghan Villages," Memorandum for Record (Unclassified), January 17, 2013, Response Memo.pdf.

5. Mark Moyar, ALP Study, February 2014, 90.

6. Assistant Secretary Sheehan, SASC Afghanistan testimony.

7. Bolduc, "Impact of Pulling U.S. SOF from Afghan Villages," 2013.

8. NSOC-A VSO-ALP Report, 1.

9. Personal interview with Ben Moeling, Senior State Department Representative and Director of the Kandahar PRT, Kandahar, June 2010.

10. Personal interview with Tom Baltazar, Senior USAID Representative and Deputy Senior Civilian Representative, Regional Command South, Kandahar, Afghanistan, June 2010.

11. I made this observation of all RC South VSO sites during the 2010 and 2011 growing seasons when community-based agricultural initiatives in VSO platforms were at their peak. I was the VSCC-South Director and USSOCOM Lead during this time with unprecedented access to reporting and economic development measures of performance and effectiveness.

12. Lisa Saum-Manning, "VSO/ALP: Comparing Past and Current Challenges to Afghan Local Defense," p. 8, December 2012.

13. U.S. Department of Defense, "Report on Progress Toward Security and Stability in Afghanistan," October 2011.

14. Seth A. Shreckengast, "The Only Game in Town: Assessing the Effectiveness of Village Stability Operations and the Afghan Local Police," *Small Wars Journal*, March 27, 2012, http://smallwarsjournal.com/jrnl/art/the-only-game-in-town-assessing-the-effectiveness-of-village-stability-operations-and-the-a.

15. BG Don Bolduc, "The Critical Importance of Afghan Local Police in the Overall ANSF Security Strategy," NSOC-A, 2013, p. 2.

16. Phone interview with Dr. Seth Jones, July 1, 2013.

17. Schreckengast, "The Only Game in Town," 2012.

18. I base this observation on hundreds of interviews and feedback on thousands of surveys from operators, conventional military, interagency members, and academia lauding the VSO approach and Joint SOF Academic Week as the best vehicle they have ever seen for bringing disparate groups together on Afghan stability issues.

19. Personal interview with First Secretary Zach Harkenrider, Office of Political Military Affairs, U.S. Embassy, Kabul, May 2010.

20. LTG(R) Michael Flynn, remarks to Threat Day audience, Washington, D.C., January 8, 2015.

21. These game changer framework chapters will go deeper than any book has ever gone on these topics. However, for local practitioners and advisors, many of you will want excruciating detail, tactics, techniques, and procedures. Not to worry: our Stability Institute has exhaustively recorded game changer best practices and

methodology tools from all over Afghanistan and beyond. If you are interested in rolling your sleeves up and getting after it at the local level, you'll want to check out the Stability Institute website (www.stabilityinstitute.com).

Chapter 7: Getting Surrounded (Village Stability Operations)

1. Captain Dan was one of only four SOF leaders who returned to the same community during the VSO era. This is a major shortcoming that should be fixed in future interventions. Grass-roots stability work in honor-based clan areas depends heavily on relationships. Rather than rely on some arbitrary organizational rotation schedule for moving SOF and other advisors in and out of contentious areas, home-station units should do a much better job of analyzing where local leaders have worked successfully and endeavor to return them to those areas. The handful of operators who did return to the same community accelerated their gains during their return trips by leaps and bounds above their peers who were trying to work their way into a skeptical community for the first time. Relationships are key and they must be empowered by senior leaders.

2. I considered modifying the term Village Stability Operations to Community Stability Operations. It seemed at first to be more appropriate since we've established that going local applies to more than just rural villages. In the end, I decided not to change it, because I don't think any of us are ready for yet another name change in an already complex arena. Most folks recognize VSO and can make the connection to its community focus.

3. Personal interview with Captain Jeremy Schwendeman, Civil Affairs Detachment Commander, Village Stability Platform in Kandahar Province, Afghanistan, August 2010.

4. Interview with Captain Alex, North Kandahar Province VSO site, August 2010.

5. Dr. David Ellis, "Building Village Governance Capacity," The Stability Institute, 8. http://stabilityinstitute.com/stability-productsbuilding-village-governance -capacity/.

6. Dr. Khan Idris, "Jirgas: Pashtun Participatory Governance," Tribal Analysis Center, Williamsburg, Virginia, 2009.

7. Dr. Thomas Barfield and Neamatollah Nojumi, "Bringing More Effective Governance to Afghanistan, 10 Pathways to Stability," *Middle East Policy* 4 (Winter 2010): 4.

8. Ibid.

9. Personal interview with Navy SEAL District Augmentation Team (DAT) Representative to Panjwaii District, Kandahar, Afghanistan, 2011.

10. Interview with Major Tyler, District Augmentation Team Representative, Kandahar, Afghanistan, 2011.

11. Francisco M. Hernandez, "An Application of Foreign Internal Defense through Civil Affairs Operations in the Upper Huallaga Valley, Peru," *Small Wars Journal*, October 27, 2014, http://smallwarsjournal.com/jrnl/art/an-application -of-foreign-internal-defense-through-civil-affairs-operations-in-the-upper-hu.

Chapter 8: Meet Them Where They Are — Embracing Local Realities

1. Steve Thomas, "From Small Unit Leaders to Rugged Diplomats: Overcoming the Tactical-Strategic Divide in U.S. Foreign Policy," *Real Clear Defense*, June 3, 2014, http://www.realcleardefense.com/articles/2014/06/03/overcoming _the_tactical-strategic_divide_107252.html.
2. Local realities emerged as we continued to define the situation on the ground in rural Afghanistan. As designers and implementers of the VSO methodology, we needed a way to characterize the local conditions that needed to be addressed and worked within, not changed. Local realities began to emerge as a common term at Joint SOF Academic Week and in several VSO training venues.
3. U.S. Special Operations Command, "Forging the Tip of the Spear," SOCOM 2020, www.socom.mil
4. Akbar Ahmed, *The Thistle and the Drone: How America's War on Terror Became a Global War on Tribal Islam* (Washington, D.C.: Brookings Institution Press, 2013), 48.
5. John C. Hulsman, *To Begin the World Over Again: Lawrence of Arabia from Damascus to Baghdad* (New York: Palgrave-Macmillan, 2009), 78.
6. Personal interview with Captain Jeremy Schwendeman, Civil Affairs Detachment Commander, Village Stability Platform in Kandahar Province, Afghanistan, August 2010.
7. Lieutenant General Michael T. Flynn, Captain Matt Pottinger, and Paul D. Batchelor, *Fixing Intel, A Blueprint for Making Intelligence Relevant in Afghanistan*, Center for a New American Security, January 2010.

Chapter 9: Extreme Collaboration: It Takes a Village and a Network

1. Linda Robinson, *One Hundred Victories: Special Ops and the Future of American Warfare* (New York: Public Affairs, 2013).
2. This data output is from Professor Diamond's negotiation class taught to over 2,500 special operators during 2013–14. His research is part of the overall body of research done at Wharton Business School and contributes to *Getting More*, his negotiation bestseller.
3. Brian Calvert, "The Merry Pranksters Who Hacked the Afghan War," *Pacific Standard*, July 1, 2013,
4. John F. Schmitt, "A Systemic Concept for Operational Design," Air University Press, http://www.au.af.mil/au/awc/awcgate/usmc/mcwl_schmitt_op_design.pdf.
5. Interview with director, Village Stability Coordination Center (VSCC)–South, Kandahar, Afghanistan, 2011.
6. John Arquilla and David Ronfelt, *Swarming and the Future of Conflict* (Arlington, Virginia: RAND Corporation, 2000), http://www.rand.org/pubs/documented_briefings/DB311.html#download.
7. Spirit of America, *Operational Overview*, October 2013, 10.

8. Dr. David Jacobson, professor at the University of South Florida and Stability Institute advisor, coined the phrase "reduces transaction costs" at the original Stability Institute Board meeting in Tampa, Florida, 2013.

9. Ori Brafman and Rod A. Beckstrom, *The Starfish and the Spider: The Unstoppable Power of Leaderless Organizations* (London: Penguin Books, 2006).

10. Seth Godin, *Tribes: We Need You to Lead Us* (New York: Portfolio, 2008), 1.

11. Jared Diamond, *The Third Chimpanzee for Young People, On the Evolution and Future of the Human Animal* (New York/Oakland: Seven Stories Press, 2014).

Jared Diamond, *The World Until Yesterday, What Can We Learn from Traditional Societies?* (New York: Penguin Group, 2012). I used Diamond's work in *The Third Chimpanzee* on the arrival of modern man to establish roughly how long man, as we know him, has been around, and Diamond's work in *The World Until Yesterday* to illustrate that despite how long modern man has been on the scene, the tendencies of contract society haven't been around that long. This is further amplified by Diamond's own words that we have been traditional far longer than we have been modern. This is a very important distinction when conducting self-analysis of how we operate in status society and even within for the purpose of this particular section, how we operate in contact society. Our status society roots affect us and inform our behavior in a big way, even if we aren't aware of it. This will create tremendous opportunity in the chapters that follow.

12. This phrase came from BG Scott Miller when he stood up the collaborative network for VSO in Afghanistan. I have since made this phrase the core mission of the Stability Institute in its efforts to build and unify collaborative stability networks all over the world.

13. Brafman and Beckstrom, *The Starfish and the Spider*, 94.

14. John C. Hulsman, *To Begin the World Over Again: Lawrence of Arabia from Damascus to Baghdad* (New York: Palgrave-Macmillan, 2009), 67.

15. Brafman and Beckstrom, *The Starfish and the Spider*, 97.

16. Ibid., 96.

17. I also pull this data point from the research body and presentation of Professor Stuart Diamond in his SOF negotiations classes from 2013–14.

18. Godin, *Tribes*, 5.

19. William Bratton and Zachary Tumin, *Collaborate or Perish! Reaching Boundaries in a Networked World* (New York: Crown Publishing Group, 2012), 597 (e-book).

20. The "Network Built on Trust" was highlighted by the USSOCOM chief of staff in a SOCOM Command presentation to the Special Operations Medical Association Conference, December 14, 2013.

Chapter 10: Lead with Story

1. Personal interview with Doyle Quiggle, February 8, 2015.

2. Jeffry R. Halverson, H.L. Goodall, Jr., Steven R. Corman, *Master Narratives of Islamic Extremism* (New York: Palgrave Macmillan, 2011), 13–14. All three definitions (story, narrative, and master narrative) come from this work and seem to

be consistent definitions from the contributors at the Center for Strategic Communications. I chose these distinct definitions in order to give better structure to stability practitioners dealing with the complexities of extremist influence.

3. *Out of Their Heads and Into Their Conversation: Countering Extremist Ideology*, by Angela Tretheway, Steven R. Corman, and Bud Goodall, Report #0902, Consortium for Strategic Communication, Arizona State University, September 14, 2009.

4. Halverson, Goodall, and Corman, *Master Narratives of Islamic Extremism*, 14.

5. Pamela Slim, *Body of Work, Finding the Thread That Ties Your Story Together* (New York: Portfolio Penguin, 2013), 185.

6. Steve Rose, "The ISIS propaganda war: a high-tech media jihad," *The Guardian*, October 7, 2014, http://www.theguardian.com/world/2014/oct/07/isis -media-machine-propaganda-war?CMP=share_btn_link.

7. The Storytellers website, http://www.thestorytellers.com/who-we-are

8. Daniel H. Pink, *A Whole New Mind, Why Right Brainers Will Rule the Future* (New York: Riverhead Books, 2006), 114.

9. Harrison Monarth, "The irresistible power of storytelling as a strategic business tool," *Harvard Business Review*, March 11, 2014.

10. Rose, *The Guardian*, October 7, 2014.

11. Monarth, *Harvard Business Review*, March 11, 2014.

12. Dr. Thomas H. Johnson and Kevin L. Steele, "The Taliban Narrative," in *Narrating The Exit From Afghanistan*, ed. Steven Corman (Tempe, Arizona: Center for Strategic Communication, 2013), 71–98.

13. Halverson, Goodall, and Corman, *Master Narratives of Islamic Extremism*, 21.

14. Johnson and Steele, *Narrating the Exit from Afghanistan*, 71–98.

15. John Anderson, "The Enemy as Hapless Clown: Abderrahmane Sissako on the Jihadists in *Timbuktu*," *New York Times*, January 23, 2015, http://www .nytimes.com/2015/01/25/movies/abderrahmane-sissako-on-the-jihadists-in-timbuktu.html.

16. Doyle Quiggle, post-deployment interview and deployment notes, 2013.

17. Ibid.

18. There is a body of open source reporting from Yemen, Pakistan, and Afghanistan, which demonstrates even in areas where extremists leaders are killed from drone strikes and surgical raids, there are large-scale second- and third-order effects with local populations expressing overt dissent and resistance to the U.S. and host nation governments for conducting these attacks. Afghan poems, known as *Landays*, are often written about drones. Several reports indicate that Yemeni tribes in the vicinity of drone strikes, who were previously indifferent to Al Qa'ida presence, are trending toward increased support of extremists, as highlighted in the book *The Thistle and the Drone*.

19. Eliza Griswold, *An Introduction to Afghan Landays*, Poetry Foundation, 2013, http://www.poetryfoundation.org/media/landays.html#intro.

PART III: INTO ACTION

Chapter 11: Bypassing the Graveyard

1. Personal interview with Dr. Ted Callahan, RC North, Afghanistan, October 1, 2014.

2. Akbar Ahmed, *The Thistle and the Drone, How America's War on Terror Became a Global War on Tribal Islam* (Washington, D.C.: Brookings Institute Press, 2013), 4.

3. Steve Thomas, "From Small Unit Leaders to Rugged Diplomats," *Real Clear Defense*, June 3, 2014, 2, http://www.realcleardefense.com/articles/2014/06/03/overcoming_the_tactical-strategic_divide_107252.html.

4. Ibid.

5. Dr. Mark Weiner uses this term regularly in his book *The Rule of the Clan* to describe modern societies versus society of status, which describes honor-based clan societies.

6. COL Donald Bolduc, "Impact of Pulling U.S. SOF from Afghan Villages," Memorandum for Record (Unclassified), January 17, 2013, Response Memo.pdf.

7. Personal interview with Henry Ensher, U.S. Department of State, Regional Platform South Senior Civilian Representative, Kandahar, Afghanistan, July 2010.

8. Personal interview with Afghan National Army Special Forces NCO, VSO site in Kandahar Province, 2010.

9. I base this observation on numerous interviews with individual trainees and advising ANA Special Forces in the schoolhouse and in combat. I would ask a simple question: "What is the mission of the ANA SF in post-2014?" I received wildly different scatter from all parties on this role. By contrast, almost all advisors could clearly articulate the role of commandos and other Afghan strike forces. The amount of energy, resources, and clarity invested in the strike forces versus the ANA SF is indicative of our lack of appreciation of Afghan realities, namely the importance of working in the rural areas.

10. These comments were from a USAID representative during a personal interview in Kabul, Afghanistan, May 2014. The field representative's name is being protected due to ongoing operational activities but the representative is well known and respected in the SOF and stability community.

11. Personal interview with Captain John, Village Stability Platform in West Kandahar Province, 2010.

12. This is a paraphrased quote from videographer and filmmaker Jim Burroughs, who produced *Shadow of Afghanistan* (2012), a compelling video documentary on Afghanistan over the last several decades.

Chapter 12: No Respite: Islamist Violent Extremists in the Homeland

1. RJ Rinehart, "Terrorism Fears Drive More in US to Avoid Crowds," Gallup Online, June 20, 2017, http://www.gallup.com/poll/212654/terrorism-fears-drive -avoid-crowds.aspx.

Chapter 13: Conclusion

1. Both of these young men were returning to Ukraine soon after our conversation, so I opted to keep their names out of the sourcing notes. The interview was informally captured after my lecture at Wharton Business School on October 31, 2014.

BIBLIOGRAPHY

"Afrighanistan? The real danger is the world turns its back on another poor place." Unsigned editorial, *The Economist*, January 26, 2013. http://www.economist.com/news/leaders/21570704-real-danger-world-turns-its-back-another-poor-place-threatened.

Ahmed, Akbar. *The Thistle and the Drone: How America's War on Terror Became a Global War on Tribal Islam*. Washington, D.C.: Brookings Institution Press, 2013.

Alex, Capt (surname withheld). Personal interview with the author. North Kandahar Province VSO site, Afghanistan, August 2010.

Anderson, John. "The Enemy as Hapless Clown: Abderrahmane Sissako on the Jihadists in *Timbuktu*." *New York Times*, January 23, 2015. http://www.nytimes.com/2015/01/25/movies/abderrahmane-sissako-on-the-jihadists-in-timbuktu.html?_r=0.

Arquilla, John, and David Ronfelt. *Swarming and the Future of Conflict*. Arlington, Virginia: RAND Corporation, 2000. http://www.rand.org/pubs/documented_briefings/DB311.html#download.

Azoy, Whitney. Personal interview with the author. Savannah, Georgia, October 2012.

Baddorf, Zack. "OP-ED: Don't Forget the Whole Point of the Syrian War — to Get Rid of Bashar al Assad." *War Is Boring*, October 23, 2014. https://medium.com/war-is-boring/op-ed-dont-forget-the-whole-point-of-the-syrian-war-to-get-rid-of-bashar-al-assad-3697e1412919.

—. Personal interview with the author. Tampa, Florida, November 10, 2013.

Baker, Pauline. "Unraveling Afghanistan." *The American Interest*, December 19, 2013. http://www.the-american-interest.com/articles/2013/12/19/unraveling-afghanistan/.

Baltazar, Tom. Senior USAID Representative and Deputy Senior Civilian Representative, Regional Command South. Personal interview with the author. Kandahar, Afghanistan, June 2010.

Barfield, Thomas, and Neamatollah Nojumi. "Bringing More Effective Governance to Afghanistan: 10 Pathways to Stability." *Middle East Policy* 4 (Winter 2010).

BBC News Africa. "Mozambique profile." Accessed October 11, 2014. http://www.bbc.com/news/world-africa-13890416.

"Bin Laden: Goal is to bankrupt U.S." *CNN World*, November 1, 2004. http://www.cnn.com.

Bolduc, Col Donald. "Report on Progress Toward Security and Stability in Afghanistan." Washington, D.C.: U.S. Department of Defense, October 2011. http://www.defense.gov/pubs/pdfs/October_2011_Section_1230_Report.pdf.

—. "Impact of Pulling U.S. SOF from Afghan Villages." Special Operations Memorandum for Record (Unclassified), January 17, 2013. Response Memo.pdf.

—. "The Critical Importance of Afghan Local Police in the Overall ANSF Security Strategy." NSOC-A, 2013.

Brafman, Ori, and Rod A. Beckstrom. *The Starfish and the Spider: The Unstoppable Power of Leaderless Organizations*. London: Penguin Books, 2006.

Bratton, William, and Zachary Tumin. *Collaborate or Perish! Reaching Boundaries in a Networked World*. New York: Crown Publishing Group, 2012.

Burroughs, Jim. Director, *Shadow of Afghanistan* (feature documentary). Cinema Libre Studio, 2012. http://www.shadowofafghanistan.com/index.htm.

Callahan, Ted. Personal interviews with the author. Kabul, Afghanistan, June and October, 2014.

Calvert, Brian. "The Merry Pranksters Who Hacked the Afghan War." *Pacific Standard*, July 1, 2013. http://www.psmag.com/books-and-culture/the-merry-pranksters-who-hacked-the-afghan-war-60873.

Carter, Shan, and Amanda Cox. "9/11: The Reckoning — One 9/11 Tally: 3.3 Trillion." *New York Times*, September 8, 2011. http://www.nytimes.com/interactive/2011/09/08/us/sept-11-reckoning/cost-graphic.html.

Carter, Stephen, and Kate Clark. "No Shortcut to Stability." Chatham House, December 15, 2010. http://www.chathamhouse.org/publications/papers/view/109545.

Central Intelligence Agency. *The World Factbook*. https://www.cia.gov/library/publications/the-world-factbook/geos/mz.html.

Clark, Howard. "Consonance in Stability Operations." The Stability Institute, November 1, 2012.

http://stabilityinstitute.com/wp-content/uploads/Consonance-in-Stability-Operations.pdf.

Coghlan, Tom. "The Taliban in Helmand: An oral history." In *Decoding the New Taliban*, edited by Antonio Giustozzi. Oxford: Oxford University Press, 2012.

Collins, Joseph. "The Rise and Fall of Major Jim Gant." *War on the Rocks*, April 15, 2014. http://warontherocks.com/2014/04/the-rise-and-fall-of-major-jim-gant/.

Community Alliance for Safety and Peace. *For Our Future/Para Nuestro Futuro*. http://future-futuro.org/en/about-casp.

Crawford, Neta C., and Catherine Lutz. "Costs of War." http://www.costsofwar.org.

Dafoe, Allan, and Devin Caughey. "Honor and War: Using Southern Presidents to Identify Reputational Effects in International Conflict." 5http://citation.allacademic.com/meta/p_mla_apa_research_citation/4/9/9/1/4/pages499145/p499145-5.php.

Davis, Maj Ian. Special Operations Liaison Officer to Peru working under the U.S. Country Team. Personal conversations with the author. Lima, Peru, June 2014.

Diamond, Jared. *The World Until Yesterday, What Can We Learn from Traditional Societies?* New York: Penguin Group, 2012.

—. *The Third Chimpanzee for Young People, On the Evolution and Future of the Human Animal.* New York/Oakland: Seven Stories Press, 2014.

Diamond, Stuart. *Getting More: How You Can Negotiate to Succeed in Work and Life.* New York: Crown Business, 2012.

—. Special Operations negotiations classes. Fort Bragg, North Carolina, 2013–14.

Dupree, Louis. *Afghanistan.* Princeton University Press, 1973.

Ellis, David. "Afghans have forgotten how to farm." USSOCOM Academic Week training program, Fort Bragg, North Carolina, June 2011.

—. "Building Village Governance Capacity — An Operational Design." The Stability Institute, 2012.

http://stabilityinstitute.com/stability-products/building-village-governance-capacity/.

—. Personal interview with the author. Tampa, Florida, October 22, 2014.

Encyclopedia Britannica. Accessed May 16, 2014. http://brittannica.com/EBchecked/topic89139.caliphate.

Ensher, Henry, U.S. Department of State, Regional Platform South Senior Civilian Representative. Personal interview with the author. Kandahar, Afghanistan, July 2010.

Fahim, Kareem, and Suadad Al-Salhy. "Exhausted and Bereft, Iraqi Soldiers Quit Fight." *New York Times*, June 10, 2014, A1.

Flak, Agnieszka. "Electricity only reaches one in three Afghans." Reuters, January 9, 2012.

Flynn, Lt Gen Michael. Remarks to Threat Day audience. Washington, D.C., January 8, 2015.

Flynn, Lt Gen Michael T., Capt Matt Pottinger, and Paul D. Batchelor. *Fixing Intel: A Blueprint for Making Intelligence Relevant in Afghanistan.* Washington, D.C.:

Center for a New American Security, January 2010. http://www.cnas.org/files/documents/publications/AfghanIntel_Flynn_Jan2010_code507_voices.pdf.

Gehrke, Joel. "Terrorists Handbook." *National Review Online*, August 29, 2014. http://www.nationalreview.com/article/386728/terrorists-handbook-joel-gehrke.

Gene, Maj (surname withheld). Personal interview with the author. Fort Bragg, North Carolina, April 2014.

Girowal, Nadir Khan. Personal interview with the author. Ghazni Province, Afghanistan, May 20, 2014.

Giustozzi, Antonio. *Koran, Kalashnikov, and Laptop: The Neo-Taliban Insurgency in Afghanistan.* New York: Columbia University Press, 2008.

Godin, Seth. *Tribes: We Need You to Lead Us.* New York: Portfolio, 2008.

Grau, Lester W. *The Bear Went Over the Mountain: Soviet Combat Tactics in Afghanistan.* Washington, D.C.: National Defense University Press, 1996.

Griswold, Eliza. "Can General Linder's Special Operations Forces stop the next terrorist threat?" *New York Times*, June 13, 2014. http://www.nytimes.com/2014/06/15/magazine/can-general-linders-special-operations-forces-stop-the-next-terrorist-threat.html?_r=0.

—. *Introduction to Afghan Landays.* Poetry Foundation, 2013. http://www.poetryfoundation.org/media/landays.html#intro.

Halverson, Jeffry R., H.L. Goodall, Jr., and Steven R. Corman. *Master Narratives of Islamist Extremism.* New York: Palgrave Macmillan, 2011.

Harkenrider, Zach, First Secretary, Office of Political Military Affairs, U.S. Embassy, Kabul. Personal interview with the author. Kabul, Afghanistan, May 2010.

Hernandez, Francisco M. "An Application of Foreign Internal Defense through Civil Affairs Operations in the Upper Huallaga Valley, Peru." *Small Wars Journal*, October 27, 2014. http://smallwarsjournal.com/jrnl/art/an-application-of-foreign-internal-defense-through-civil-affairs-operations-in-the-upper-hu.

Hulsman, John C. *To Begin the World Over Again: Lawrence of Arabia from Damascus to Baghdad.* New York: Palgrave Macmillan, 2009.

Human Rights Watch. *Just Don't Call It a Militia: Impunity, Militias, and the "Afghan Local Police."* New York: Human Rights Watch, September 2011. http://www.hrw.org/sites/default/files/reports/afghanistan0911webwcover.pdf.

Idris, Khan. "Jirgas: Pashtun Participatory Governance." Williamsburg, Virginia: Tribal Analysis Center, 2009. http://www.tribalanalysiscenter.com/

Ignatius, David. "Drawing down, but still projecting power." *The Washington Post*, March 29, 2013. http://www.washingtonpost.com/opinions/david-ignatius

-drawing-down-but-still-projecting-power/2013/03/29/591ebe30-9895-11e2
-814b-063623d80a60_story.html.

International Crisis Group. "Afghanistan: The Problem of Pashtun Alienation."
Asia Report 62 (August 5, 2003): 4.

Ismati, Tariq. Deputy Minister, Ministry of Rural Rehabilitation and Development,
Afghanistan. Personal interview with the author. Savannah, Georgia, October
2012.

Jacobson, David. Personal interview with the author. Washington, D.C., February 7, 2014.

J.D., Special Forces NCO who helped start the first Nagahan VSO site in
Arghandab District, Kandahar Province and eastern Afghanistan. Personal
interview with the author. Fort Walton Beach, Florida, 2014.

John, Capt (surname withheld). Personal interview with the author. Village Stability Platform in West Kandahar Province, Afghanistan, 2010.

Johnson, Casey Garret. "Afghan Islamic Courts: A Pre-Taliban System with Post-2014 Potential?" *New York Times*, April 17, 2013. http://
atwar.blogs.nytimes.com/2013/04/17/afghan-islamic-courts-a-pre-taliban
-system-with-post-2014-potential/.

Johnson, Thomas H., and Kevin L. Steele. "The Taliban Narrative." In *Narrating
the Exit from Afghanistan*, edited by Steven Corman, 71–98. Tempe, Arizona:
Center for Strategic Communication, 2013.

Jones, Seth, and Arturo Munoz. *Afghanistan's Local War: Building Local
Defense Forces*. Arlington, Virginia: RAND Corporation, 2010. http://www.rand
.org/pubs/monographs/MG1002.html.

Jones, Seth. Personal interview with the author. Washington D.C., June 2010.

—. USSOCOM briefing, Tampa, Florida, May 2011.

—. Phone interview with the author. July 1, 2013.

Justin, Lt Col (surname withheld), Director, Village Stability Coordination Center–South. Personal interview with the author, Kandahar, Afghanistan, 2011.

Kilcullen, David. *Out of the Mountains*. Oxford University Press, 2013.

Lala, Haji (name changed). Personal interviews with the author. Savannah,
Georgia, October 2012 and December 2012.

Laster, Maj Gen James, USSOCOM Chief of Staff. SOCOM Command presentation to the Special Operations Medical Association Conference. Tampa,
Florida, December 14, 2013.

Long, Austin, Stephanie Pezard, Bryce Loidolt, and Todd Helmus. *Locals
Rule*. Arlington, Virginia: RAND Corporation, 2012. http://www.rand.org/pubs/
monographs/MG1232.html.

Maher, Shiraz. "New 'Manifesto' Shows al-Qaeda Learning from Mistakes." *ICSR Insight*, February 15, 2013. http://icsr.info/2013/02/icsr-insight-new-manifesto-shows-al-qaeda-learning-from-mistakes/.

Maylie, Devon, and Daniel Gilbert. "Anadarko's controversial Mozambique project shows appetite for natural gas, Endeavor could cost tens of billions of dollars far from viable customers." *Wall Street Journal* Online, August 11, 2014. http://online.wsj.com/articles/anadarkos-controversial-mozambique-project-shows-appetite-for-natural-gas-1407810602.

McMillin, Kelly, Chief of Police, Salinas Police Department. Ride-along field research and personal interviews conducted by the author. Salinas, California, October 2014.

Mead, Walter Russell. "The Evolving Terror Threat." *The Wall Street Journal*, March 4, 2013. http://www.wsj.com/articles/SB10001424127887323829504578272033024365110.

Merriam-Webster Online Dictionary. www.merriam-webster.com/dictionary/collaborate.

Moeling, Ben, Senior State Department Representative and Director of the Kandahar PRT. Personal interview with the author. Kandahar, Afghanistan, June 2010.

Monarth, Harrison. "The irresistible power of storytelling as a strategic business tool." *Harvard Business Review*, March 11, 2014.

Moyar, Mark. *Village Stability Operations and the Afghan Local Police*. JSOU Report 14-7. MacDill Air Force Base, Florida: Joint Special Operations University, October 2014. http://jsou.socom.mil/JSOU%20Publications/JSOU14-7_Moyar_VSO_FINAL.pdf

Mukhlis, Hatem. Phone interview with the author. October 23, 2014.

Nabi, Mohammed (name changed to protect against retribution). Personal interview with the author. North Kandahar Province, Afghanistan, January, 2010.

Name withheld. Afghan National Army Special Forces NCO, VSO site in Kandahar Province. Personal interview with the author. Kandahar, Afghanistan, June, 2010.

Name withheld. Director, Village Stability Coordination Center–East. Personal interview with the author. Bagram Air Base, Afghanistan, February 2011.

Name withheld. Director, Village Stability Coordination Center–South. Personal interview with the author. Kandahar, Afghanistan, February 2011.

Name withheld. Economic Development Representative, Village Stability Coordination Center–West. Personal interview with the author. Herat, Afghanistan, February 2011.

Name withheld. Navy SEAL District Augmentation Team Representative to Panjwaii District. Personal interview with the author. Kandahar, Afghanistan, February 2011.

Name withheld by request. Senior officer, military planning division, U.S. Embassy, Baghdad. Personal interview with the author. Baghdad, Iraq, October 2014.

Name withheld. Senior USAID OTI program manager. Personal interview with the author. Kabul, Afghanistan, May 20, 2014.

Name withheld to prevent retribution. Tribal leader and former Kabul national security staff, and cultural advisor to Special Operations Forces. Personal interview with the author. Kabul, Afghanistan, May 20, 2014.

Name withheld. Village elder. Personal interview with the author. Maiwand District, Afghanistan, September 2010.

Names withheld. Two Ukrainian citizens studying at The Wharton School. Personal interviews with the author. The Wharton School, University of Pennsylvania, October 31, 2014.

Niemand, Riaan. Personal interview with the author. Cape Town, South Africa, October 22, 2014.

Obama, President Barack. Commencement address. United States Military Academy at West Point, New York, May 28, 2014.

Odierno, Gen Raymond T., Gen James F. Amos, and Adm William H. McRaven. "Strategic Landpower: Winning the Clash of Wills." U.S. Army, U.S. Marine Corps, and U.S. Special Operations Command White Paper, 2013. http://www.arcic.army.mil/app_Documents/Strategic-Landpower-White-Paper-28OCT2013.pdf.

O'Leary, Carole. Near East South Asia Center for Strategic Studies. Phone interview with the author. October 23, 2014.

Open Society Institute and the Tribal Liaison Office. "Strangers at the Door; Night Raids by International Forces Lose Hearts and Minds of Afghans." Kabul Open Society Institute/Tribal Liaison Office, Kabul, 2010.

Phillips, David. Personal interview with the author. Washington, D.C., July 2013.

Pink, Daniel H. *A Whole New Mind, Why Right Brainers Will Rule the Future.* New York: Riverhead Books, 2006.

Quiggle, Doyle. Email interview with the author and deployment notes. Stuttgart, Germany, February 8, 2015.

"Rio Tinto to sell Mozambican coal assets." *Business Day Live.* July 30, 2014. http://www.bdlive.co.za/africa/africanbusiness/2014/07/30/rio-tinto-to-sell-mozambican-coal-assets.

ROBIN SAGE, culmination exercise for the U.S. Army Special Forces Qualification Course held at Camp MacKall, North Carolina. This unconventional warfare exercise spans multiple counties and towns in rural North Carolina, incorporating these areas and their population into a role-playing war zone of Pineland. During this exercise, Green Beret students learn to link up with, train, and advise partisan guerrillas against a superior conventional force.

Robinson, Linda. *One Hundred Victories: Special Ops and the Future of American Warfare*. New York: Public Affairs, 2013.

Rose, Steve. "The ISIS propaganda war: a high-tech media jihad." *The Guardian*, October 7, 2014. http://www.theguardian.com/world/2014/oct/07/isis-media-machine-propaganda-war?CMP=share_btn_link.

"Rural Development and Counter-insurgency: A Case Study." FAF Development. Kandahar, Afghanistan: 2009, 8–9.

Saum-Manning, Lisa. "VSO/ALP: Comparing Past and Current Challenges to Afghan Local Defense." Arlington, Virginia: RAND Corporation, December 2012. http://www.rand.org/pubs/working_papers/WR936.html

Scheuer, Michael F. "Al-Qaeda in the Islamic Maghreb (AQIM): Using crime to advance Salafist goals, secure safe havens, and acquire international reach." Tribal Analysis Center, January 2015. http://www.tribalanalysiscenter.com/Research-Completed.html.

Schwendeman, Capt Jeremy, Civil Affairs Detachment Commander, Village Stability Platform in Kandahar Province, Afghanistan. Personal interview with the author. Kandahar, Afghanistan, August 2010.

Schmitt, John F. "A Systemic Concept for Operational Design." Maxwell AFB, Alabama: Air University Press, 2006. http://www.au.af.mil/au/awc/awcgate/usmc/mcwl_schmitt_op_design.pdf.

Sheehan, Michael, Assistant Secretary of Defense for Special Operations. Testimony on Afghanistan to the U.S. Senate Armed Services Committee. Washington, D.C., May 16, 2013.

Shreckengast, Seth A. "The Only Game in Town: Assessing the Effectiveness of Village Stability Operations and the Afghan Local Police." *Small Wars Journal*, March 27, 2012. http://smallwarsjournal.com/jrnl/art/the-only-game-in-town-assessing-the-effectiveness-of-village-stability-operations-and-the-a.

Slim, Pamela. *Body of Work, Finding the Thread That Ties Your Story Together*. New York: Portfolio Penguin, 2013.

Sochurek, Howard. "American Special Forces in Action in Viet Nam." *National Geographic*, January 1965.

Spirit of America. *Operational Overview*. Los Angeles, California, October 2013. https://spiritofamerica.net/index.php.

The Stability Institute. www.stabilityinstitute.com.

Stewart, Rory. "Afghanistan: 'A Shocking Indictment.'" Review of *No Good Men Among the Living*, by Anand Gopal, *The New York Review of Books*, November 6, 2014.

Stigall, CSM J.R., Senior Enlisted Advisor, Combined Joint Special Operations Component Command – Afghanistan (CFSOCC-A). Personal interview with the author. Kabul, Afghanistan, June 2010.

The Storytellers. London. http://www.thestorytellers.com/who-we-are.

Thomas, Steve. "From Small Unit Leaders to Rugged Diplomats: Overcoming the Tactical-Strategic Divide in U.S. Foreign Policy." *Real Clear Defense*, June 3, 2014. http://www.realcleardefense.com/articles/2014/06/03/overcoming_the_tactical -strategic_divide_107252.html.

Tretheway, Angela, Steven R. Corman, and Bud Goodall. *Out of Their Heads and Into Their Conversation: Countering Extremist Ideology.* Arizona State University: Report #0902, Consortium for Strategic Communication, September 14, 2009.

Trey, Capt (surname withheld), former Arghandab VSO Commander. Personal interview with the author. Fort Walton Beach, Florida, February 2014.

Tyler, Maj (surname withheld), District Augmentation Team representative. Personal interview with the author. Kandahar, Afghanistan, February 2011.

Tyson, Ann Scott. *American Spartan: The Promise, the Mission, and the Betrayal of Special Forces Major Jim Gant.* New York: Harper Collins Publishing, 2014.

Ucko, David. "Clear, Hold, Build, Fail? Rethinking Local Level Counterinsurgency." *War on the Rocks*, November 7, 2013. http://warontherocks.com/ 2013/11/clear-hold-build-fail-rethinking-local-level-counterinsurgency/.

U.S. Census Bureau. *United States Census 2010*. Washington, D.C., 2010. http://www.census.gov/2010census/.

U.S. Special Operations Command. *SOCOM 2020: Forging the Tip of the Spear.* MacDill Air Force Base, Tampa, Florida: USSOCOM Public Affairs Office, 2013. http://www.ifpa.org/confrncNworkshp/confrncNworkshpPages/socomOct2013/ USSOCOM%202020.pdf.

—. *Special Operations Forces Operating Concept.* May 2013. https://fortunas corner.files.wordpress.com/2013/05/final-low-res-sof-operating-concept-may -2013.pdf.

Verizon Wireless commercials, 2002–2011.

Weiner, Mark S. *The Rule of the Clan.* New York: Farrar, Straus and Giroux, 2013.

Williams, Phil. "Alternative Governance in a World Without Order." Lecture to Threat Day audience, Washington, D.C., January 9, 2015.

Withnall, Adam. "Inside ISIS: The first Western journalist ever to be given access to the 'Islamic State' has just returned — and this is what he discovered." *The Independent*, December 21, 2014. http://www.independent.co.uk/news/world/middle-east/inside-isis-the-first-western-journalist-ever-given-access-to-the-islamic-state-has-just-returned--and-this-is-what-he-discovered-9938438.html?origin=internalSearch.

ABOUT THE AUTHOR

D. SCOTT MANN is a retired Green Beret Officer with over 22 years of Army and Special Operations experience around the world. He has deployed to Ecuador, Colombia, Peru, Iraq, and Afghanistan. Scott is a Senior Fellow with the University of South Florida and the CEO of Rooftop Leadership. Scott regularly speaks to and trains corporate leaders, law enforcement, and special operations forces on best practices for going local and making better human connections. Scott has frequent appearances on Fox News, CNN, and other national platforms as a thought leader on countering violent extremism, building organizational relationships, and restoring trust in our communities.

Scott lives in Tampa with his wife and sons.

Scott invites you to stay connected on this journey to change the game:

Website: Rooftopleadership.com

Facebook: Official Scott Mann

Twitter: @realscottmann

Instagram: Rooftop_Leader